KONPARA :

A COLLECTION OF SHORT POEMS

KONPARA:
A COLLECTION OF SHORT POEMS

Dr. N. Narasimha Ramayya

Prints Publications Pvt Ltd
New Delhi

Published by

Prints Publications Pvt Ltd
Viraj Tower-2, 4259/3, Ansari Road,
Darya Ganj, New Delhi-110002
Tel. : +91-11-45355555
Fax: +91-11-23275542
E-mail : contact@printspublications.com
Website : www.printspublications.com

First Edition : 2022 (Hardbound)

ISBN: 978-81-948490-8-7

Price: ₹ 1295/-

Published and Printed by Mr. Pranav Gupta (Director) on behalf of Prints Publications Pvt Ltd, New Delhi.

Preface

Spiritual delight in KONPARA, where venus is bright, beautiful and delightful on a mass for performance on the work of a deity. It can bring about a racial or social change though anonymity is predominantly sprightful. Hence this brief anthology of poems so powerful so akin to each other in expression. May be it is a depiction of sportful comics as a challenge to the world of innocence and approximation. "The world is well lost" and yet it lasts forever that what the commandors can do not as rapscallions but as soldiers to fight for *dharma.* Yet there is no parlance in the common parleys.

Candidness is the watchword of democracy in the place called KONPARA and people in general, live and die for it as in Indian doxology, demonology and hegiology. The ensuing poems in this collection, no doubt, never ty to supercrede the other and hence it is all about a spiritual reality till or lasts, the truth as a gift of God all for goodness. Mostly, the contrivance could be for the sustenance of phenomenology, epistomology and ethics. Some of the poems have been eminently depicted to emulate the inner meaning as the core of unrevealed manifestation. Hence, any great artiste could have done the save in KONPARA pittance is the costly truth of guidance. Hence, this poetry. Most of the Indians are not useless fellows.

Dr. N. Narasimha Ramayya

Postscript

"Poetry is the criticism of life" and as I know, that Dr. N. Narasimha Ramayya sustains it and elevates it. He is a theorist as a writer and poet well known to the world of critics across the world.

Konpara is symbolic India and the world at large with a back drop of *Venus of Konpara* by John Masters. The technique the poet uses is the objective correlatives and auditory imagination. All the poems are in the metrical free verse and thematically it is all about the unrest of the post-modern literary world while the poet loiters in a three fold circuit : lamination, animation and culmination. Consequently *Konpara* might suggest a solution of remedy though evanescent at present.

In the Indian ethos Venus, is Goddess Lakshmi and tended by the Greek mythology and more so, any beautiful heroine of modernity—subdued and empounded. I understand the poet has seen the Queen of beauty only once in the work-a-day world and never more. Yet Konpara could be a Venus of Hoisalas, Pallavas, Chalukyas and the like as an epitome of aesthetics and the idea of blood consciousness. In either case the grandeur is the work of *Konpara.*

There is challenge of change and it is a gift of God and inevitably, latent : the idea of flesh minus Sigmund Frend. The poetic beauty is in the immortality of this work.

The hero is the poet himself. The setting is the present Global earth and the green-room is incongruity governed by the poet's own chequered life.

Dr. Ramayya is a foster child of the English language.

N. Vani

nadamuniv@yahoo.com

I
Kanaka Tara

Kanaka Tara, a golder star,
Self-imbued, self poised,
A self-willed power,
Like a distant relation,
The Venus of Konpara,
Mitigates, mutilates,
Indian minds unselfish,
Look as the star gazers.

Imbued and undued,
Love is with no love there,
Like monosyllabic words,
or radical fests of zest,
Pawning and fawning,
Mutual funds pester,
No scuttling for chinks,
Hereafter no sigh even,
Paddy is safe in the field.

2
Figment

Figment as fitful fever,
Labyrinthine embraces in,
Like cosmetics and costumes,
Costly or fastly feast at,
Dogged as dreadful death,
A phase in fazed enormous,
As in endless cosmos,
Folly functions firm,
Fusion is for infusion.

As friends with no funds,
And enemies as with trends,
Confused defusion as such,
Plateau to Plato platonium prevails,
Like a patent plethore behoves,
Eftsoons festoons ring out,
And seasons are sinister,
As if premonition funks.

3
Fragment

Infusion and confusion,
Like a chalice of malice,
Demonstration and remonstrance,
To cash, bash, lash, gash,
Mash and smash as trash,
India that is Bharat,
No anarhy no discipline,
In God's name please.

Like the spiritual delight,
Casuistry lampoons one and all,
No encumbrance whatsoever,
For prosaic poem or so,
Smutty and guilty sanctum,
As statutory remarks,
No Bharat bund for today,
Or subterfuges at the most,
Some plenary session at least.

4
A Heist

A heist as robbery nobody knows,
What's what in the offing,
For abnormal obsessions,
Subnormal concessions,
Like the vulnerable torso,
Coffin can decide the fate,
To go to hell or not,
Heist is the gist altogether.

In a terbnacle of elves,
Like a haunting egoism,
Weaker spoils do not come,
The migrating etiquette,
In the passing moonlight,
Night awaits none,
Impasse is greater,
The blue margin of the sea,
That might succumb to it.

5
Bull-fight

Bull-fight or ram fight excels,
The emeralds and mileage,
Like mortgaged lineage,
Sentient and sententious,
Lack of spirit that extols,
God feeds the bull and man alike,
(No sophistry is there),
Battlements or batty fellows.

Or bosom friends and castenets,
Like Stallions strong enough,
No faltering for caskets,
Big fools fight for a light or sight,
Swallows can hallow,
And the pot-boilers do well,
To hold the placards to know,
But hellucinations pilfer,
The noble ideoms so to speak out.

6
God Forgives

So as to signify something strange,
Like unicorn or popcorn,
Or even speechless rhythm,
Forlorn as miasma neglect,
Neologisms and archaisms,
Or even the village politics,
Be speaks to speak out,
God forgives all the hooligans.

Every spook or every crook,
The strident poet writtes,
Like progressive digression,
Emigration to immigration,
Kalaedoscopic downfall,
As in endemic dudes,
Nudes and trades alludes,
We apologise as denizens,
And He forgives us all.

7
Portent

So to tell off or not to tell off,
A reprimand perse,
Like a benign persona,
The hassocks are undue,
Like carsandias portent,
No Dido but dude,
Shrewd and stealthy,
The concept prevails.

Sexy glamour glows,
As a photostat copy,
Like persmified beauty,
and a spontaneous raga,
Live in a courier, Bonsoi,
Or soldout sex,
Sans-for, sans-lay, sans-joy,
A portending manuscript,
That ends in the pangs.

8
Indian Colours

Puckering bickerings,
As in love and romance stern,
Of pickadilly circus,
Kamathipura gallies,
Cave in or pave the way,
But no satire un attire,
Like sash or sashaying,
As God protects us all.

As in caverns or aqueducts,
Colours differ in India,
Like a varying similarity,
Panacea and poison are safe,
Spokes are in the wheel,
And the hub being in the centre,
Congruent or incongruent,
Semblance as resemblance,
Or even for social security.

9
A Poser

No sagging or ragging,
For the fleshy curves (fleshy?)
Like the booming billows,
Of the Philistine race asunder,
Only to extirpate them,
Mephistopheles is those,
Not a subnormal fellow,
With a pathetic panygeric.

As in equimarginal returns,
There is no expunge yet,
Like a platoon commander,
There chief withstands the animosity,
Frankincense smears the truth,
Apogees are ever alive,
Solemnity is a grave result,
Plight dooms itself,
May be it is a genre.

10
Healthy Stealth

Like a healthy stealth,
Innovators work hard,
A stubble of corn cut,
Or gangrene overpowers,
And emphasis is on the grave,
Graveyard and wineyard,
The symbiosis is enough,
For most hungry looks,
Dubbed to death.

Defence ends the match,
Like the spenserian stanza,
Prowess can save one and all,
Or sometime bonanza,
Rapidcity as an eternal force,
Placards and blackguards,
Imply and comply the avowal,
Reply can swear in the force.

II

Process Forever

Howling and seowling scrappy,
Like learning and earning foppish,
Gangsters alone can do happy,
Winter the harbinger of fowls,
Fools and mules aplenty,
Equanimity and hyperbola,
Just like the palanquin heaven do,
And we worship the warships.

Toadies alone can do wonders,
Long live revolution of candrer,
Like spontaneous relativity,
Lends or ends the cashewnets,
Internets as amalgamated,
Cancels only to mend or fend,
Tender in the nightfall,
As in someone's grave,
God is a continuous process.

12
Toadies

Gandy toadies as Indian goatees,
Of Boira caves and caves are,
Like snaky and foxy fellows,
Frenzied in enzymes,
Torch the torch bearers,
Footage and fitment,
Laconic as lampoons,
Never speak out truth.

As in a tardy chime,
Sporadic tempers cleave in,
Like nastalgia as the end,
And untouchable lerity,
As the rollcall of death,
No alegorythms but a pattern,
God saves us all,
The toads and toadies,
Ah! materialistic world.

13
Modernity

The silver coinage or beverage,
Marks the modernity a new,
Like spoilage of acreage,
Ebullient nature still empowers,
Yasmin or Jasmine the same,
Power cut in the dark den sultry,
Dragged into the cases and beaten up,
India that is Bharat!

No culminating fulmination,
Uproar is havoc though,
Indian minds can cheat or beat,
Like self praise addicted to,
Almost bon voyage!
A piece and anon,
As atheistic apothecaries,
Fragile fecundity,
Fasts and lasts.

14
Undertaken

At times you can rot or trot,
Or even rap the prop,
Like seance at thrill,
Middle class morals seamy,
With a strong memory,
Everyone as an undertaker,
But throldom stalls ambiguous,
Trenchant sabotage malls.

Mewd or spewed, lewd or shrewd,
Indian make in a brand new,
Like bull in spell bound trance,
And no morale in ghetto,
Skeleton in the cupboard,
A family skeleton as in norms,
And bizarre runways strange,
Strong foothold makes shrine,
No more in the long departure.

15
A Malady

Something is bracing or charing,
Like an undertrial case,
I am no longer a voice now,
A fragmentary element lost,
Singing with no bringing effect,
As a henchman follows till hell,
With no hub or spoken as rungs,
I can trace the grace.

Like white ants and coconut trees,
As sarcaperilla that innovates,
Not a bandit queen to die at last,
Freezing and squeezing,
Vast subjects of age old history,
Character is destiny not always,
Testy fellows annoyed,
Tether themselves to the hype,
Most charactered Indians.

16
Delusion

Sober is the sobriety with acumen,
Delusive illusion as democracy,
No line of control in it,
Like no prevarication per se,
Peevish, rakish, mockish,
Pansies grow every time then,
Agenda is the love lorn programme,
As percusions effect the repercussions.

No disarray alone but confusion also,
Modifies the embodiment,
As to reform or conform,
The hopeless hapless fey future,
Like a claimant's cause,
And the futurist is God,
Spinoza for Delusion or so,
Menu, mileu and epoch,
Or panchayat elections.

17
Morale

No king canute nor the Danube even,
Can set right mankind,
So no clientele,
Percution ensobled,
Like no danger persisting,
We preach morals, morale,
And diction strange,
Or bold peasantry.

Chengiz Khan, Kubla Khan,
No Hitler, no Mussolini,
Like the war lords asleep,
History perpetiates perpetual,
Though marking nuts are plenty,
To make the marks, sharks,
Larks, larvae and the states,
Gives us indomitile courage,
Or the musical background.

18
Divine Life

We speak truth forever,
As the angels do or wisest fools,
Or to protect or protest,
Like a divine life later on,
"Forever, and forever",
"Fir wrangling queen"!
That disputes salvation,
The divine queen credible Moksha.

Phase is the goal as mace,
Like a spouting gorgoyle,
As in searching summer,
"Summer surprised us",
Human life as suspended,
Sinks, funks, with all its kinds,
Thought it blinks, winks as sphinx,
No more a sordid boon,
It is cheerful mode.

19
Horrid clime

Man speaks though bleak,
Like an uncertain creak,
Or some sound and fury,
Till the death is a fancy,
A horrid clime, shine or rime,
"Slow and steady wins the race",
Then the emerald glows,
Shines, of sinful mines.

People dye their hair,
Only to spy the sky,
Or to die or lie,
Like war mangen as harbingers,
Nallifying mellifluous,
Hindu culture agogtrenchant,
A dance drama with a crisis,
And a speedy disposal,
Baroque and burlesque, lewd.

20
Showers

Premonsoon showers,
To defeat the heat wave,
Like an endearment outsourced,
And the swallows swing swiftly,
The bleak hope enveloped,
The small brains fulminate,
Perhaps the fulsome love,
Smears and bears the truth.

We discover nothing new,
Brahman is always there,
Let us appease to suppose,
Like no myriad souls apart,
Land of scarcity or aplenty,
From devilry to adultery,
Retrieve the showers,
Some platonic concept to crisis,
The upholstery changes a lot.

21
Veracity

Manifest or unmanifest, God is great,
Silt or kilt there is no tilt,
Like God's grave unproved,
As in conformity with information,
As sporadic veracity,
No vindictive vindication,
For a philistine race,
Ambush in no end.

Some double edged sword fights,
Tight, might, light to fight,
Like a kite or an eagle,
Luxurient luxury of nature,
Mature, stature and fulsome,
Pedagogy entails the truth,
Lamentation is no end,
Blinds protect the windows,
Endowments and candoures.

22

Peace

Embryonic natural phenomena,
No mindset is yet,
I have lived my full life,
Like aseality hovering,
Some instrumentation abstract,
No huddle of bookies now,
As if pragmatic paranocia,
Overtakes the regimentation.

Ego-conscious, blood conscious, and
In the cemeterical region as well,
Many vistas, vibes and vignetter,
Like the vindication of vendetta,
Earned to learn and spurn,
Adormant format finesse,
No fuddling of meddle yet,
Almost a quagmire,
Vigilent translucent.

23
Pleasure

Man is selfish not woman,
Loyal man and disloyal woman,
Like modern Devdas or Majnu,
Sex, love and non-sense,
Poems lays or elegies,
Venus, Aphrodite, Cupid, Eros,
And bohemian out,
Can start the mart.

Abnormal sex and normal penis,
That befits the irritale vagina,
Like a symbol of Konpara,
Venus as a side symbol of Goddess,
Is not much to enlighten us,
And gallows in the end perhaps,
Symphony as the decorum,
Is a peep or beep for a keep,
And that is the pleasant end.

24
Grass

"A snake in the grass" is sneky,
Sneaks, speaks, curtly, smartly,
Like the throes fluffy,
To befit plagiarism,
Link and sink all together,
Some disease for delight,
That escapes no escapism,
Drifting for the shifting current.

Fucking the licking sickness,
Astronomy as blizkrieg,
Like the formless superiority,
Not besmeared fornication,
In a formless house,
Or a Camelot afar,
Enseasoned with langerse,
Depiction of eviction as tiffs,
Of eventful history.

25
The Countryside

Some wretches and some bitches,
Smartly alleviated,
Like uneasy stretch or stench,
For no rehabilitation;
Indian morals as enduced,
The world moves on yet rotates,
Gall is a fall or a mall,
That encumben one and all.

He shrinks, she expands,
That is stealthy life then,
Like habitude ignored,
Or situation eschewed,
Dispensation enumerated,
Nature pervades no stress and strain,
For improviation or cavil,
Some enticement yet remains,
The countryside is green.

26
Mango Grove

The ratrace and the hattricks,
Mish-mark as melancholy,
Like cavil regretting,
Some mishap awaits further,
Free love, free style wrestling,
Or miniature painting,
Brook no tirade,
As in a mango grove.

I Love English and live for it,
Two mangoes on the English chests,
Like glamour spoken to,
Or even marjorams do,
Nastalgia rings out,
Fatalist fantasy fancies,
A Falstaff is safe forever,
And feminine cillade,
Is as if endangered.

27
Enemies

Sincerity is lacking,
People are smacking,
Rocks are cracking,
Like porcupines are whacking,
Yet we are not idle to track,
But we might jokes to crack,
I am emotional and to face,
So as to the enemies deface.

Heraldry embraces hunting,
Like a gas stove the flame,
No mildness at all in rural life,
People sooth or see the enough,
Peony is there pleny is also there,
To end the impasse regular,
Phrases and Idioms great they are,
To send or bend or even to tend,
The disaster and all that.

28
Pleasantries

Pleasantries and countryside,
Unseamingly great,
Like a unique cardomum,
Unambiguous authority,
As the Indian barks of crises,
Pride rules no land,
How I and how do I write?
As a sufferer to suffer.

A shred in for strain,
Brain sprain or grain,
Like a burlesque tone,
Or castles in the air never,
Lascivious but castigated,
Or rather cartrated to funk,
A bunk to clink,
Ethered clime at hand,
Or a cardoned respect.

29
A Buff

The most wretched sciety wonderful,
I live in to pray to God,
Why to inform, why to perform,
Like the synthetic fabrics,
Winning and cunning sobriety,
Monopoly of manouvring,
An ibex for buff or muff,
A stealthy puff or buff,

Like intenecine decency,
That vents the incursions,
Most inhuman race of devils,
No Sancho Panja lives wholesome,
The pantheon is for panthers,
As of spoken on written English,
I write for myself now,
And no pedigree of evils,
To write an absurd history.

30
Maze

"Sleep, baby sleep"
Beep! beep!! beep!!!
As in the sprawling meadows,
Lafargue and animals,
Like cadmium and chemicals,
And in tender splendour,
Lazy and hazy maze,
This is the way of world.

As in laburnum grove,
Like a phase to graze in,
To praise or raze on,
Something like razzmatazz,
Chilled penury of the livestock,
Or even Palam airport,
Clinched or clenched,
The airport can be safe,
Right man doesn't say morals.

31
Demeanour

No sludge is hereafter,
Man is a sluggard,
Like the site in for sight light,
Might, kite and slight,
Haggard is blackguard,
Only vanguard is left out,
Something mandatory or bondage,
No catwalks any more.

They go for showers, bowers,
Lovers, who don't shiver,
Like no vibrant lethargy or so,
Indian minds harm others;
Vanquished votaries,
No changing in for checkmates,
Some vituperation yet,
Vestiges promptly worn,
Demeanous is the end.

32
Surrealism

Verbosity to verbiage,
Animosity and diversity,
Like love ringing, singling, clinging,
The ship sails, hails and fails,
May be Indian secularism,
Sanctum, phantom, quantum,
And municipal visions,
Good riddance to bad rubbish.

Sagacity to velocity,
Veracity to eradication,
Like a heart pumping or jumping,
Fulminates skipping to draw flak,
Only to uproot the bonsai,
This is endearment,
As an environmental speed,
Chimpanzees do well,
It is no alacrity perhaps.

33
Chaos

Frigid girls are many,
Like rigid belles, stills,
With no luminous bodies,
Spousy pairs of chaos,
Uncertainty prevails,
Sarcastic gaseous stimuli,
No incest, but zest, fest,
And rest to test the mutiny.

Like subdued encounters,
As suppressed truth,
Miasma creates mangles,
And the combustible substance,
Brings in ingredients,
Facile flames and conflagration,
The braided trade unions,
Brace up and face-off,
For no eternal glory.

34
Psychotherapy

Cheeky women are saucy,
They make husky talks,
Like the broiled puffing,
No Aurora, nor Hesperus,
Lousy or drowsy dawn,
Can tangle the eve,
From serenity to senility,
We whack or sack others.

This is enough for the day,
Justice remains at the end,
Like a melce that captures,
No fray when they bray,
And a psychopath has no path,
When selfless love manouvres,
Man prays to God in vain,
A mental strain to over come sprain,
For a psychic treatments.

35
Belief

It's all but nonsense to believe,
To perceive and to receive,
Or even to deceive before hand,
As in likewise similarities,
Like the cloudy skies gather,
Amnesty can respre greatness,
Fakeness, meekness, likelihood,
Speechless rhythm as contour.

Spacecraft as state craft,
And to raise the gambits,
Like Indian tamarind sour,
No bitterness acclaimed,
A coward's end is Howard's end,
Calamitous is the progenetor,
Juicy is lucious succulent,
And the CABAL Ministry is safe,
Be it British or India.

36
Go Getters

An antelope with an antler,
Like an alabaster semi-prescious,
No row for measurements whatsoever,
This is the way of life astir,
No exciting rapprochement,
A prismatic precision,
Some molestation at the end,
There is no afar encroachment.

In a land of setters,
We are go-getter with fetters,
Like the lassitude enamoured,
With no encroachments but blitz,
Blitzkreig and symposiums,
Assented liabilities the body shrinks,
Of the elite and the laity prolific,
Some light hearted levity,
Amity or spoken English.

37
Man's Psyche

No supernovas hereafter,
But only grand canyons,
Like no supercilious thoughts,
My memory is still alive,
And the Almighty protects me,
The approach road is short,
As much as a melancholy string,
Favour unfavours us all.

Man an apostate angel,
Is an apostle for no war pact,
Like the political peace maker,
A pacifist, a Gandhian,
A messenger of conch shell,
Or Phillips radio lost,
A spasm as a nutshell,
As in doyen township,
No much difference at all.

38
A Boss

No longer mopping or moping,
Only yapping and fopping,
You can toss for a boss,
Like a metaphysical prowess,
A communal boss or a lass,
Toppling and wrangling,
A mother tongue or lang,
A paradigm to sting.

Trance in a glance,
A lancer can do a little,
Like the prepositions alike,
Irony of fate that rules out,
Seizure is a cinecure,
Or else a cessation,
Humanity is for devilry,
Of course, a heavy toll,
Or else a campfire.

39
Wonders

Doodle and the noodle,
Like a dude as the nude,
Girdle is for the cradle,
Some glamour, some armour,
A corslet can do wonders,
The niche for the rich,
To pick up the gauntlet,
So is the case for India.

Oddities as demeanor,
Soil erosion and erasing,
Like an exposure unlimited,
Recount the countless enmity,
Accreditation as usual,
Pave the way for star wars,
Man is the meanest animal,
For animals never rattle,
Battle unlike the cattle.

40
Detachment

Viragos fight for mirage,
No vigil but vigilance for,
Watch and word democracy,
Vignette as the period of life,
Like self-immolation detested,
Jargon besets askanee,
A fuss for detached outlook,
As a qualified job.

Detached, detrimental,
Like the cutpiece, cut motions,
Or democratic doodles,
For aping and gaping to escape,
A samurai is a shogun,
Who can smudge not to budge,
Full of dudgeon and smoke,
Stealthy utensils,
Simplicity and nonsense.

41
Scenario

Parochial sporadic decrees,
Every thief is great,
Like a teat that is good,
Roses and prim roses do not fight,
As diversified factors,
Trenchant penchant scenario,
Deliverance is ever good,
But the device is the end.

Constant reverse as a venue,
Selfish man focuses the land,
Like a dittoed temperature,
The sun and the moon shine,
Or glow to dethrone the spasm,
Embankment is enough,
Man is again a devil,
Religion can save him,
But could it be devastation.

42
Ferrets

Dent or dint is the goal,
Or else prickly peas aghast,
Turret is there, ferret is there,
Like a safeguard ignored,
Frenetic no doubt creates fun,
Quandary is at times uncertain,
Tour de force can be a skill got,
Lay off gives a little reprieve.

The idea of flesh is no good,
It takes you to the other man's wife,
Like a subaltern aimless,
Fiendish but jumping note,
Pregnant thoughts foresee business,
Man made ideals and guats,
As for mutual attraction,
Imagery or savagery,
Or for mutilations.

43
Kites

Kites for bites glitch make,
No disorder out of order emerges,
Like pessimistic optimism,
As pragmatic dogmatism,
Foibles of human nature,
Supplicates the simplicity,
That is enough for mite,
Moity and hoity-toity.

Pomp is romp of scamp,
We are mad after fame,
Like the lame and blind,
With no formidable fests,
I write to forget myself or to forge,
Barge, large, gorge and to sip,
No accountability hereafter,
Since the party wins to lose,
We want the lion's share.

44
Amazons

Amazons are a few,
To raze the wretchedness,
Like the spiritual overgrowth,
And the logicians are simple,
Correct English for the boors,
Incorrect and unEnglish filth,
And smilthy grows and grows,
Only to hobnob the truth.

Silly hobbled boys smirk,
No lay out to demarcate,
Like an overture turned out,
Or overweening self-confidence,
That perches the smirch,
Not to confound the comity,
Of the beauteous ideas,
Unscheduled and undeduced,
No blot is analogous.

45
Ageing Cage

Ageing cage in the body,
Lost the aplomb almost,
Like the disappointment,
Rowdy elements and paramours,
Rowlock and gunwale,
The boat barks in the sun,
Or capsized a man of straw,
It sinks in the least.

Grace can chase at base,
Like rhetoric, a figure of speech,
A chapman as Il Penseroso,
Heavy blows of rows with no end,
As in a disappointed lyric,
Phase one as a guard,
No labyrinthine forage, footage,
As a forum of perplexity,
A forensic forum.

46
This Life

This dirty body moves on with,
Slips, lips, hips and tips,
Like a bumper crop indeed,
Munera Pulvaris,
Pros and cross breed,
Or Alcasian dogs, sparriels,
Bumper crops sashaying,
But no tithering yet.

This is life spiced,
Fruitful but negligent,
Like spasmodic convulsions,
Gaurdy spirit and lively,
Embezzled toll tax,
Meandering ramification,
Slooping, not sleeping,
Enigmaic simplicity,
Slobbering and slashed.

47
Odds and Ends

If littered up with odds and ends,
It is tittered and glittered,
Like the Brahmin's smile,
Guile, bile or file,
Writers as fighters, lighters,
Ignite, percolate and permeate,
Fig for straw! or braw!!
Simple folks laugh at them.

Sprights are tight now,
Spend the rift nature is sick,
Like ends are odd forever,
An end paper at last,
At large thieves remain,
No longer highway men amain,
They may clink or link,
Sophomores are no more,
In India that is Bharat.

48
Hammock

No bullying further hereafter,
No hammock for the rest,
They hamper and scamper,
Dramatic irony for levity,
Like the visitors visionary,
Memento as in recitation,
And the decisive virus,
Can also change the computer.

Seasonal trasmutation,
Like a berrish turmoil,
For transfiguration sceptical,
Nothing in abject in Nature,
Transcendence foils the theme,
Seasdogs are historic unique,
Mystery is as pastry or a spook,
Sometimes prompt compliance,
Indians are coolies abroad.

49
Fraternity

Heart is safe but not mind,
No, the other way round,
King Caphetna swore a royal oath,
Like style in the man,
No appalling endenance,
Roaming on a gala day,
Eschew the fraternity,
Only to defray the calamity.

Transsexual ambience,
Defrays the dichotomy,
So as to under seore or not,
Of sentient I am able to perceive,
Things, subtleties, encomiums,
A fraction of eternity as God,
Like the pyramid prismatic,
Some refraction foretells,
The comic is as usual secret.

50
Bachchus

Bachchus in aglow,
When drinking is not over,
Like a camouflage that threatens,
Man's mind in active,
Bachchus thrives,
When man lives for God,
Somnambulistic half sleep,
Seizure the measure.

Impressive prosperity,
Like no evangelism aghast,
An egoist and egotist quarrel,
Some coiffure for coherence,
Emasenlated person is manly,
Once again as in Dutch courage,
Scottish free and frenel leave,
As duteous bedrock or wedlock,
Besmeared with no hedgehog.

51
Saddle

No panoply nor girth,
(Neither Girtha nor Wamba even),
As specialities first and last,
Girdle the saddle round,
Afar, across and alike,
As in a symposium serious,
Severity political very much,
Now adden dam almost.

He is a stalker perhaps,
A priori amenities pursued,
Like the enough questioned already,
Yet something is plausible,
'Death lays his hands on kings',
Nobody is in the saddle then,
Till a mushroom growth overhails,
Piqued in a peevish way,
A horse is not a stallion.

52
Triumph

Divine cell unimaginable,
Ambrosian approach,
For a filly's grave,
Like mannerless ill health,
Yet there is something great,
Unemployed easement,
Groterqueness undefined,
A pineapple juice almost.

A collegian colloguy,
To topple the rabble-rouser,
Like a filligree work emvalued,
Disapproval for the approval,
Some mackintosh laid upon,
And the dogdays are ahead,
At last molecular biology,
No wretch can be alive,
Olive is a sign of triumph.

53
Probity

Probity goes to the sun and the moon,
That's for amelioration,
Like a searty rainfall,
Unauthorised guarantee,
And love is saddled anyhow,
No severance henceforth,
Allelujahr can decide the factor,
As a brandished new thing.

A trenchant struggle,
No percentage of gimmicks,
Like the midnight revels,
Or even in the promenade,
Solicitous so firth similar,
Indian politics of gogetters,
Adjudged as the best test,
Lest we should lose or muse,
When we choose the devil.

54
Catcalls

Not a comity or errors,
But an odyssey almost,
Like a comedy of errors,
Or at least an eat out,
Only for cut and thrust business,
To simplify to amplify,
"Age cannot wither her",
And at last poetry to catcalls.

Enervation that smothers,
Like smelting the raw oar,
As in a sweltering heat,
Occurence is common for greed,
Meed, creed, seed to breed,
Brain wash is the end of outfit,
Taliban force is curious,
Rapid vapid or at the insipid,
Stupidity prevails over all.

55
Money

Witches, bitches, stiches,
Riches, matches, batches oh!
Like no seamy side for scaring,
Seance is perhaps the end,
I have done my duty for a bend,
And when you tend to lend money,
Estuary is eerie, a plover,
Or alive like cockroaches.

No Indian can speak untruth,
For it is blood speaks for him,
Like the litigation elusive,
A stalker is a stockist,
Let me remain skeptical,
And nobody is very honest,
As lazy fellows are too many,
Yet intrepid gestures evoke,
Gangsterism or cannibalism.

56
Petty Thieves

We are for takers and makers,
Or even for lockers and crackers,
Like the female smackers,
But at times slack and crack,
Thieves of the Indian blood,
No more lackadaisical,
Depend on largesse or burgess,
Simple scenario sound syndrome.

Feigned madness, deigned combustion,
Fact finding familiarity,
Like death after death afar,
Or at the most a synthesis,
Some mythical reality,
Drought and famine,
That make man devout,
Tremulous or stimulus,
Either is flamboyant.

57
Character

Character is Destiny,
But not in India or elsewhere,
Like an excessive heritage,
Or even psychotherapy,
Mordant health of mobidity,
Checkered or puckered,
Some cliché is andent,
Poignant in everything.

Simplicity as metrology,
Fecundity as usual,
Like superficial syllogism,
Pshaw! Perdu!! and mischief,
Hidden psychosis of perdition,
No character assassination,
Lascivious castigation,
Prejudiced with firmness,
And no pejorative purpose.

58
Seasons

Moody foodies as teddy bears,
Eschewed as in a gargoyle,
Like a scimitor, a proof,
For omnivorous animals,
Uncandry and superlative,
Strange mysterious sepulchre,
But prelude to nonsense,
I write for myself as usual.

Nothing is strewn in the humans,
No more landgrabbing etc.,
Like the political upheaval,
The dormitary is safe,
Despite the road accidents,
Human treasure can cope,
Some pathetic fallacy,
Or landscape unknown,
Almost hopeless seasons.

59
Metrology

A system that funks,
Of measures and weights,
Like subsumed scoop,
Or a senttle as stilt,
A noble style for stile,
That licks the irony of fate,
A plane of no plain water,
At least on Michael Mars.

No benchmark for trafficking,
Or at the most a showcause notice,
Like the scores settled,
Of undescored scamp,
Trap, scrap, rap,
Teasing or freezing the test,
The element grows rampount,
Though a rake it is fake,
May be an animal feeling.

60
Horseshoe Magnet

"Sex is superior to life",
Mahnoor and Kohinoor apart,
Were above Taj,
No naustalgia before or beyond,
Like a master piece upheld,
Apart, above or below,
There's placement overall,
Neither to overhaul nor to can.

Day to day is God's law,
Endevour or cashewnuts,
Like the embryo discovered,
Nothing is more or less,
Every individual is gentle,
And India is all the great,
Ample, sample steel plant,
Kirdremukh is no longer heart,
Horseshoe magnet know? (no?).

61
Suffragette

Suffragette steals the show,
Of suffrage, as euphoria,
Like the enphimism exalted,
Simple melancholy pensile,
Age old days of the past,
As in the war time imprint,
Nothing but sad diadem,
Can ignore persons for softness.

Someone as mentally ill,
Grossness as structure,
Like fame exists fumes,
Seasonal change for things stand,
A unique case as dignified,
Some blatant truth yet perturbs,
The disturbance is usual,
Common catastrophe levied,
Levity is nothing indeed.

62
Get Away

Belfuj is a clock tower,
Made of chance, timely malice,
Like Godly pandaemonium,
Or ethereal encirclement,
For a minimum breakthrough,
A spendthrift cult grows agog,
And occasioned gewgaw,
That succumbs to no end.

A geyser is also a getaway,
Like an escapist submits,
In a celler undue,
No compassionate nemesis,
Could gradually blow up,
Caesarian operations,
Play up and pay up,
An obeisance made for,
Amenable compromise so far.

63
Recognition

Hotch-potch, topsy timmy,
Higgledy piggledy, and nonsense,
Everyone is great in this world,
For nobody is smaller,
Hearsay, gainsay,
Spherical, sleepy, half-mast,
All is political rivalry,
Chaos, sturdy, lonely,
A bush is a stubble,
Bubble, rubble huddle,
Hail Hitler, God swearing.

Some neologism is logical,
Buggies and beggary permeating,
Like India is always great,
No carnival, but carnage,
Or *dharna* only to earn fame,
Cognition of recognition.

64
A Peek

A quick look that is enough,
A peak that looks beyond,
Like a good Samaritan aloft,
No duplication all the same,
Despite the disquitude is calm,
For a sporadic stylist infact,
"Anon, anon we cry",
As if the fox howling.

An infinite holding above,
The style is a jargon at present,
Like anamolous indication,
Indictment is angry soon,
Of amateur artist(e),
Or intermittant permission,
To stray and stay aghast,
Food cycle or cataclysm,
Palmistry or polyandry.

65
Duplicity

Duplicity and simplicity,
Yet people earn money,
Like the sardined small,
Blandishments as nonsense,
Sinners can swim in the abyss,
It is their hell perhaps,
A lingo, a limbo, a jumbo,
Jet fighters juxtapose.

Sinners deserves sins no shines,
God punishes them all,
Like mad rigals for andinals,
Or at least by an RTC bus,
Confession for expiation,
Catholicity brooks amity,
By a rapid force displine,
Separate electoral rolls,
Enissances can profess.

66
Samples

Scintillating corruption,
For no Indian is corrupt,
Like highwayman cry wolf,
Reservations acry fairces,
Acrimonious blasts,
Separate states, anarchy,
Dimensions, delimitations,
Operation Blue star.

Dry leaves barking in the sun,
A kingfisher is safe,
Like severity of action plan,
Every Indian is good,
And bomb blasts are casual,
No shirt for a flirt,
And the sample is ample,
Though you trample,
As a clandestine wretch.

67
Charisma

"Maurie hold on tight,
And down we went",
No more fading hereafter,
Like the shade that shakes,
Mace is safe in the fight,
For heartfelt diseases,
A voracious reader to nestle,
Peep or keep away the sorrow.

No charisma for plasma,
As in a flattened bosom,
Like insomnia relished,
Dodged and lodged to dog,
So big a fraudulence a piece,
Intimations intimidated,
Disclosed or closed fast,
The spree is almost free,
Appearance is opulent.

68
Pay-Off

No bribe but pay-offs,
Someone is almost greedy,
Needy stalwarts do see,
Like the image foregone,
No more expletives,
For the battle is won,
A steadfast globalisation,
Till Antarctica melts.

A vanguard as courtguard,
Some altercations follow,
Like a tirade put out,
No longer vanilla ice cream,
Or at least some explosives,
As the candinal virtues spoken,
And precepts one overthrown,
Build up a refrain miasma,
For condensed cadence.

69
We are Good

Now the phone culture persists,
As hot cakes or deep lakes,
Like the cloudy flakes,
Sky in the limit for elegance,
Attempting echo, pedantic,
Antique fine scenario,
Figure heads govern us all,
And call it symbiosis.

Asbestos at the best zinc sheets,
Apron clad, mad, fad,
Like toady negative,
Something as at cross-roads,
Or to read between the lines,
Estrangement at length,
Spoken are round the limb,
No ideas to ring outside,
Perchance we are all good.

70
Charlatanism

Hewn or sewn garment is the same,
For fame, shame, lame, game,
Like suzerainty overpowering,
A mate is a fate,
While in spate she can bait,
Slabbering, chanting,
Chanlatamism that cooks up,
Slammed unfamous.

Glands and hormones as well,
Like the global warming,
Sinners are siamese gloating,
Or at the most chaplains,
For faze or craze craving,
As mandering miasma,
No biggies only piggies are in row,
Aplomb they say it's good,
Safdurjung is safe yet.

71
Zealots

No blogging or clogging,
Only ragging or fogging,
Like the water flogging,
Write-ups for rights, rites,
Cataloguing rejoicing,
Lagging, tagging and ragging,
We are at loggerheads,
Bumbledom in applause.

No malcentents now in India,
When great people live selfless,
Like the prophetic godmen,
Assiduous calamitous nevertheless,
Selfdom fight they for prose,
For a poetic zeal or justice,
Prolific or platitudinous,
Sinful thoughts never come,
Though they flirt to assert.

72
Thorp (e)

Thorp (e), a village a hamlet,
A place of doldrums and not more,
Like a heavy burden on the heart,
No more dovecotes only berets,
Human seasons look them,
A link of negative positicism,
Something good or bad,
The worst is a thorp (e)

Like the lunar eclipse,
God may save the land of beggare,
Malcontents and liars,
Disorder of orderlies,
No maldries and mandates,
Toying with tassels,
Or tussle of street mongrel,
Contact number of thoubadors,
Or spousal arrangements.

73
Endless Gossip

An epicurean lunch has punch,
Nothing is officious nor bossy,
When sacrosanct to lucidity,
Like an endless gossip,
Squabbling or rambling,
Shoggy and craggy bundles,
Corroborate only to cooperate,
Squeeze and freeze together.

Neanderthal is no more,
He had no spouse that time,
120500 years before unfazed,
Immortal man continues,
Like an endless continious,
Bethink while me thinks,
An earthquake is a guardian,
For a guardian knot to cut it,
A fuss unwholesome now.

74
Tales

Sexy man feeds his sex,
With wife rife with strife,
Fairy is like Mary, chary,
To carry the tales or fails,
As in a Philistine race,
Never to face the grace,
As in Chamber of Commerce,
Lord Chamberlain can connive,

Tail lamps trace the bails,
Like obscurantism upheld,
Apprehensions as stalwarts,
Stultify the miasma,
Egocentric faith of no ego,
Cataracts over the hills,
Must shine in the spring,
A wing, ring or sing,
None is ready to tell tales.

75
Cradle

Cradles and ladles deport,
Report and escort the crayons,
Like no fazed encumbrance,
Whether you demit, emit, remit,
You are always great,
If sponsored by God,
Levity is no good at all,
Legendary binds quarrel,

Robust silk for the death bed,
Coffin or the ordeal beforehand,
Like puffed or stuffed pillows,
Surveillance unchecked,
Gloated or floated alike,
Bulging as no sedge,
A bolster that supports,
As in a Greek tragedy,
Affirm the affiance.

76
Rapture

Devoid of spell or hell,
We can smell and shell,
Like a spoiled grass,
Grotesque as a Bolshevik,
Courtesy begets courtesy,
To capture the rapture,
Crooning as cowering glee,
Spouse can wear costly blouse.

Most cunning and winning,
Are the priest class, ecclesiastes,
Like the shunning mackerels,
How do I hate India and love her?
So much as no clash enderrurs,
Shining marvellous spoonfeeding,
Elemental body a bonsai,
May be a Trafalgan square,
Raphurous moisture cloisters.

77
Assistance

The humdrum of life makes it great,
From syndrome to aerodrome,
Like replenished remains,
Broken meats or seats full,
Afar and aghast unique still,
A sequel to Raphael's diplomacy,
Unearned and uncoffined,
Enchantment is all.

Make believe stories,
Of shrews and fetishes,
Like man as fetishist,
Complex or duplex flat,
As in innovation influx,
Sunday schools are many,
And manly mannerisms,
Is for sunflower oil,
That lubricates or fabricates.

78
Avowal

Indian minds are very kindly,
Like the bortich pins,
For confessions or passions,
Eminent prominence,
Or even the alluvial soil,
Forward or wayward,
Their speech is silver,
People live only for others.

Parroting and ferreting,
The rabbits which are flabby,
Like a partime pursued,
Perturbed and disturbed,
As in a clash of Indianisms,
Threat of retrenchment,
A token of plasma miasma,
No confused infusion,
Diffused dissipation.

79
Tombstone

"The stick and the carrot",
(The threats and the bribes),
Man's hands manhandle,
Like Balticola in Sri Lanka,
Some prima-facie case,
Pristine as in woman's scars,
Stars, spars, tars, bars,
Fumes of brimstone.

A tombstone of no grimace,
As in the prison of Zenda,
Like abstractions withheld,
Bows and vows are waste,
Fumigate, religate, mitigate,
Standardised riches,
Surrender to insurrections,
Blueberries, gooseberries,
Avow as the scare crows.

80
A Scimitar

No scimitar, no scabbard,
Vigorous, rigorous emaciated,
Like a moot court enshrined,
Love is for contentment,
Endearment, skilful promptness,
Scoonful intimidation scorching,
Debris engulfing aster,
Maligned as no war time.

In this mortal world unreal,
Omniscient God alone is real,
A fairy shall marry,
Or tarry to carry,
Yet no measured treasure,
Affinity is never definite,
Merchandise is antelope,
No woman is honest in wedlock,
Although sophisticated she is.

81
Rationality

Bullocks goring the hillocks,
Publicity stunt, God, theism,
Like religion covered through crisis,
Same entellechy, no ribaldry,
Nor idolatory to reach the cemetry,
Vinegar and sinecures,
A century old calamity,
They can create famished.

Impromptu vacillation,
For rocky fellows and bonsai,
Seizure is for cessation,
Like the decay forestalled,
An enduring particle or so,
To reconnoitre semblance,
An endless end page,
At times shrewd or lewd,
St. Helene is sacred.

82
Episode

A valetudinarian image,
Any sage would present,
Like the courage posed up,
Depiction on eviction of two,
The apartheid and Banjara,
Hills stand for stills or pills,
No idea is new now,
And some episode in behind.

Episode by episode,
It is a regimen emerging,
Like economic developed,
Space travel is a must,
To reach the outer space,
Our research is for fundoos,
God gives the gift of cosmos,
Or even seance to retell,
Or the raison d'être perhaps.

83
Effulgence

Though temporary effulgence,
Man's disorder is set right,
Like the polestan unseen,
Nothing to circumvent,
Nor anything to fabricate,
We live emaciated as such,
Seizure for meameing seance,
Fabulous amount of radiance.

Some open ventriloquism,
Not to take an amiss,
... and the echo ring,
Like ambivalent ruling,
We pamper or hamper,
Stealthy lookout or so,
Pad, fad, mad, lad, bad,
A shanty built up in town,
Rogues alone can discover.

84
Apathy

Cheerful apathy sues us all,
Like besmeared caval cade,
Deteriorating end fulfills,
Speedy fazing baseless,
A male voice and a female voice,
Can together produce vices,
Major sins kins, tins,
Nefarious fellows for negation.

Indianism disconcert,
For Fulvia was perhaps great,
Like to desponate Kingfisher,
We waft and waffle wishy-washy,
Or might journey in air,
Replica of Devil apathetic,
A harmone or *ashram* life,
We travel only to baffle,
Mere to lubricate or fabricate.

85
Coquette

No grimaces hereafter,
A coquette flirtations,
Like a prude, a womanly,
Garments, dress and beauty,
Snazzy but sneaky,
Harmony that she makes,
Credential as creeking,
Freezes or breezes.

Up the creek in difficulty,
No embellished farce or so,
Like a panegyric upheld,
The praise is for craze,
The body moves with bodice,
Gloating and bloating,
Only to sashay or hearsay,
A lemonade sweet sour,
But a prudential source.

86
Revelation

As a punitive tax for parsimony,
No Indian is a scoundrel,
For the Gita was taught here,
And the Buddha was born,
Like a tangible revelation,
Parrying a ferry to mix up,
Let us call it makeover,
A tranformed fascimile.

A make believe world,
Some paroxysm at the most,
Like confounding abundance,
No formal character indeed,
Demogorgon is in danger,
Perhaps the routed simplicity,
Agile fraqility is aground,
As an anchored ship to contrive,
Relaxed are the feelings.

87
Affluence

Like a cavern of the plateau,
Hobgoblins as hobnobbed,
Affluent henchmen live,
Scramble, ramble and grab,
Seasoned one the linners,
It dies for fame or shame,
The nameless rich simplify,
The architect or the monoliths.

A fragment is a figment,
Music that you lap up,
Can sap, rap, trap, scrap,
Like a funny fumigation,
Tart or smart in the show,
Influential affluence,
As ordained in old age,
Specific scenario sinks,
So as to regain the recess.

88
Tobacco Day

Pomp Mumps are a grub,
Like plummy English,
And hot gooseberries warm up,
Tobacco puff as a buff,
Can produce rebuff,
A muff at his wits' end,
May snuff or sniff,
For Pandora's Box.

Tweedlum-tweedle dee,
Muzzy confiscation atop,
Like foiled female foetus,
That grabs or drabs or crabs,
Stealthy fundamentalists do,
Crochets and facets,
Meant for old crocks,
Spoken english as dizzy,
For facelift of freedom.

89
Shame

Shame begets no fame,
Like a crammed up line,
A hollow sham, infame,
A festered flower, lily or so,
Meet Jenifer or a pup,
Assaying and essaying,
As in a common entrance test,
A feat can hold as bold.

Reasonable reaction,
As in a flinching candle,
Like concocted dicoction,
Happiness is all decisive,
In as much splinters are there,
The groups prosper forever,
Warmth is there never,
Cogeney is for decency,
High sounding words ennoble.

90
Snarl

Like the cover design,
A dragon excels a dragon fly,
A maistiff overtaken a ceitiff,
Fantastic, egotistic,
Chaurinistic, cariola type,
Dosage can presage,
A message or massage,
Indian minds topple others.

No seowling to snarl,
Supplanted the redress,
Like destiny to destination,
Age old courtesy is good,
The type stands for hype,
A solid taranfud creeps,
The food is for breed creed,
Laxity is for tax or fax,
But sex withstands it.

91
Quelling

No writer, no fighter either,
Is lighter than the other,
Like magical imagism a flow,
The imagery impasse innovates,
The imago is fart fetched,
Fantastic evil monger,
Woman is for man, man with God,
But for the parochialism.

No imbroglio hitherto so far,
India is forever great,
Like love never ruled out,
We are in a fine land,
Though Gujjars and Meenas fight,
Call it animal quelling animosity,
Adulation is nice per se,
Plandits are fine just,
No longer confusion yet.

92
Social Service

Negative ideas for positive thoughts,
Just to blunt or pester,
The comity beyond the skills,
"All day long the noise of battle rolled",
Repletive of relativity,
Whopping or whooping,
Man excels woman to plump,
Like a labyrinthine halt.

Either crying of frying,
Prying or trying,
Like in begotten of the sole idea,
Commetocs or tomatoes,
There is doubtful elixir,
"Summer surprised us" all,
A tarnished or burnished head,
Now a salvaging point,
That's enough transcendence.

93
Village Life

Everyday I write to lament,
Or for the eternal glory,
Like the village life villianous,
Eternal glory fortified,
Village life, the country scene,
Last in the least to spill the beans,
Goitre in the end mere,
The screw is loose.

Though a disclaimer,
Reign as a king or queen,
Like a village head forthwith,
For life is short unspoken,
God is great though in dilemma,
A cataract falls from height,
Somnambulism stops the scene,
Devilry can hush up,
Some makeover for the rural Gods.

94
Frigidity

Young girls are frigid,
Old women are rigid,
Like the preemptive fragility,
To make off with (steel),
Sterile virile motile again,
Yet vignetter are simple,
And the apron casuisting flitters,
May be it is a flip-flop.

Vibes are also jibes,
Or for the opinion poll,
Gerrymandering complex,
Like the cinosure or so,
Marry first and tarry last,
It's but parsimony,
A makeshift cognizance,
Domineering women believe,
Draw flak or confluence.

95
Social Unrest

Social unrest as in dust,
Like monkeys and squirrels,
Go on squad duty for quartz,
While strong and windy,
Sombre seclusion shiny,
Strife is gone for grief,
Esoteric extinct egoism,
At times atones for extremism.

As preachers, teachers,
Indians are story tellers,
Peevish as negotiable,
Like the deliberate dealers,
Dedicated to life backbiting,
No braggart is prudent,
Refugees for skirmishes,
They scarmble or ramble,
Or at least they gamble.

96
Introspection

Every word is original,
Like every God of romp,
Simplicity as the form,
Nothing is awry to spray,
Glitz is never for blitz,
Dirty body elevate the cache,
Language as the cachet—
Prestige as the renown.

Backdrop on brainstorm,
Like an emaciated figure,
Orientation as a glow,
Peaceful unrest a piece,
There's luck unforeseen,
Destiny for destination,
Amuck as usual tomfoolery,
Aforesaid as before viewed,
A cyclical introspection.

97
Abdication

Abdication to leave out,
Of throne, crown, loan,
Like drastic erosion of asses,
Skilled as in skilful sins,
Akanee of aerobats,
God protects the devout forces,
Dismay adjudged simple,
Train of grains rumble.

Embellished as stucco or music,
One is brave or grave,
Like presaging pleasantry,
To tumble or rumble or gamble,
A turtledove tarnished though,
Tough to sniff as a buff,
Solace of circumference,
Staple food is prescribed,
Politics takes its own place.

98
Caprice

A serious muff is for trough,
Trenchant or penchant,
Gandy is the risk,
Thwarted the hearbreak,
Like the swarming images,
To mesmerise or to captivate,
Something is a navigation,
As in nastalgia.

A renegade retrogate,
None is blarphemous,
Like the sychophancy main,
A traceless objective staunch,
Spherical hyacinth curling,
Apathy to antipathy reverse,
Caprice in a great change,
Lounge, dormitory no guide,
Bride or stride is free.

99
Identity

Pave out, cave in mysterious,
Pretensions are easy,
Like the sapphire available,
Impetuosity ignored,
Indian friends are bad,
Indian foes are fine,
Nocturnal symbiosis,
Or anbunnal leaves even.

Pans and fans are amoral,
For ornamentation and plandits,
Like vagrant youths seducing,
Ejaculation is common!
A discese for self-immolation,
Gratifying truth untrue,
Defiance is for the fame,
Law and disorder at last,
The idea "I belong".

100
Orientation

On to / into a contact with,
Dissembling resembling,
To persuade or dissuade,
Like desisting resistance,
Some micobiology waves,
The great grandeur across,
The will can spill or fill,
Siblings can do well.

Sex, life and death,
To hide and slide towards joy,
Like a crown that frowns,
Indian standards muffle,
Scuffle and ruffle,
Merely miffians know,
Ah! disdainful thoughts,
Stride and abide by truth,
Once we were all great.

101
Ethnicity

Weeds, seeds beads lead us,
To zenith, beneath the glory,
Like dignity discerned,
Or ethnicity percolated,
As in guerilla warfare severe,
Sensibility in singular simple,
Bishop's seeds acrid,
Quality distinguishes.

Serene, sincere sinecurers,
Lead or mislead the world,
Like no Iraqi war or so,
Political havve is a rig,
Pan of paganism, non-moral,
No longer a Greek-god humble,
Hot cakes are sold in retail,
Hind Gods can sabotage,
Or can't even so for goodness.

102
Scrambling

Vanquished or languished—
A matter of chance,
Like an alien foody,
For eatout sportive,
In degenerated mileu,
Simplicity woos the viewer,
And no spokes of a boxing wheel,
Linger for weaving out.

The wear and tear is common,
Spinoza is away now,
Like dilapidated Konpara,
More or less Khajuraho,
Emblematic semblance,
Allegorithms for allegory,
And preparations can't fear,
When they bear the barns,
Some God sent gift!

103
Simplicity

Visuals are sacred still,
Stunt links the lamentation,
To duck down or crane up,
Like an ibex before hand,
Festoons are dear for hear,
Or the king neglected,
And forbearance truthful,
Gorgeous are the rebels.

Philosophical vacilation,
That connotes the hallucination,
Like a paragraph enriched,
And paraphrased again a verse,
Verbatim reply awaited,
A genius is a mighty deity,
But tense at times to commence,
When he cracks he attacks,
But simple splendour as true.

104
Land of Unity

Praying and straying as usual,
Nick name the land of unity,
Like prying and crying,
As seasoned sumptuous stress,
Or a blouse piece blowing,
A puppy style baying,
Hapric is the chords,
And notation brings now in.

Nabulous Neptune flickers,
In mind's miasma,
Like the fany overgrown,
Sporadic events one time,
And they end in commerce,
The worst game of antifice,
Seafarers are better then,
Thorani ailment can save,
None but to the grave alone.

105
Audacity

Gloomy clouds as cotton flakes,
In the sky float to loot,
Like the jumbo jets,
Are the war planes now,
Summer is over to trow,
Sententious is screaming,
The monsters can't mushroom,
Nonpleased in the death knell.

Culprits speak from the pulprit,
No pinching but lynching,
Like the whipping nostalgia,
Actual death is forever near,
Passage of glory is akin,
But recompulse is repulsive,
Animation brings audacity,
Our ideas are over grown,
Darkness in all.

106
Milch Buffaloes

Milch buffaloes and buffer stocks,
Can save the nation,
Like the bulbous vegetation,
Or Machiavellian tactics,
That might incongruous,
And casual myriad growth,
So also freatless felming,
Baulk no pleasure.

"You gave me hyacinths a year ago",
Villainy and heroism together,
Like a combined cupidity,
Some Venus of Konpara,
Perhaps the lion's share,
Rudeness is for wreckage,
Lucid in the tacitness,
But tranquil is the primrose,
A symbolic dove in for peace.

107
Commercial Negation

As in a stressful strain,
Sensuous and sensual,
Like compassionate passions,
Build their own pagodas,
"Mercy in not strained",
Oracle of Delphi is not heard,
Speech rhythm marvellous,
A hapsack of malice avows.

Everything is costlier,
Than the human life here,
Like the pre-judiced mermaids,
Though jovial the civic sense is,
Poignant yet it is sour,
The rift conveys concomitant,
A rare latticed greenery,
Deduced to circumspection,
May be dandruff in the end.

108
Pussy Cat

Rings bring in thrilling gongs,
Or thronging garbage,
Like universal prowess,
To dominate and domineer,
Till Fortinbras rules,
The governance as a tornado,
And a pussy cat can reign,
The oceanic range in vast.

The part is gone long ago,
And the future is aforesaid,
Like the agog cyclops,
No matter as perturbed disturbance,
Somovan is still hot,
And a dead ruffian,
Embalms the endless end,
Supposition as a belief,
Thwarts or throttles.

109
Affinity

Some mystery is there,
For cohesion, no inhibition,
Like the ancestral faith,
That circumambulates,
No verbosity for the present,
Godly perseverance somehow,
Succulent adhesive,
Skirts the virulence at last.

Like adhesive adolescence,
A youthful track is unsafe,
And the unrest is maximum,
That culminates in confluence,
Circumstantial evidence,
For introspection as such,
Liberates the soul or heart,
Candidness is not for grief,
But brief and minute insolent.

110
Scholar

Seduced to adduce,
Reduced totraduced,
Like lingerring in lounge,
Or language lopsided,
We can deduce a little,
Circumlocution can render,
That rendition is fine,
After all a phambulator!

From cradle to grave,
Babbling baby sitters belong,
Like a crumbling creche,
Snobbery better than pride,
A bride of innocence,
Periphery rules the centre,
Accidental fire toffers,
Tumbles, fumbles, grumbles,
An accomplished scholar.

III
Poetic Talent

Sometimes early or surly,
Servitude to solicitude,
Altitude to solitude,
Like the snowmansinking,
Only footpaths we know,
Or a dogguel, a mongrel,
Abletant poetic talent,
Overgrows the turpiticede.

Lassitude is harmful,
Fortitude is welcome,
Like a pastilic panoramic,
And longevity elongated,
The laudeble apprehension,
At times mortifies alas!
Quakerism is finally good,
And the end paper is subtle,
Though motile may be futile.

112
Magnitude

As in Konpara trade braided,
Grows and subsides missing,
Like solemn divinity,
Eradication still erodes,
As in an eddying pool,
No levialthan but eros tempts,
If Dian is alive for a shepherd,
A cynthia can be reveller.

Nature a strange ranger,
A forester, woodlander,
Like a splashing dasher,
Produces magnitude,
Or echoes God's voice,
"Thus the thunder spoke",
Amplitude, no lassitude,
Only but longitude,
As a unique phenomenon.

113
Chit-Chat

Venus to Pururava,
Vortex as snake power flows,
Like poetence head to foot,
Snakes tangle, entangle, wrangle,
Perhaps snake bite, might, rite,
Spherical strength stronghold,
Though in fray the prowess,
A lotus in the pond of ganglion,

Grandeur brings and clings.
No physique but spirit,
Like fantasia, consciousness,
Outer space Godly force,
A smile bequiled,
Venus is for her love,
No leading showdown,
But a daliance or sex,
Powerful recreation of Nature.

114
No Distance

No laudable distance,
The disturbed remonstrance,
As in Gorakhpur,
Like the Gita is a scripture,
Facts and fiction,
Fantasy prevails,
Phase of life demonstrates,
A diktat almost.

A fist has the fistula,
Or gusto atleast,
Like profligacy ruled out,
"Distance avails not",
Time a major factor,
Demogargon lives for all,
Perhaps Yama in our tunes,
Winds blow to dive out,
The West wind is the end.

115
Carcases

Now it's mothone,
Carcases everywhere remain,
Like abundant deaths foretold,
No burrowing but furrows,
Or the skin puckering,
We live elsewhere helpless,
Enhanced casualties,
As the roll call of death.

Fame and shame balanced,
Age for the lame,
Like Titanic forces facing,
Famished or theistic,
And wild casuarinas swing,
Sing and cling or bring about,
Appellations and rhythmic rimes,
To overcome the catastrophe,
Death closes all.

116
Penance

No seance hereafter,
We shall not perish forthwith,
Like the penance updated,
Prodigivus is the will power,
As monocotyledons can do,
A little by little grace comes,
We might need patience,
Call it indulgence original.

In a glance I can pry,
Spy, try, cry as a prig,
Lo! some wig is a Big End,
Mercuric men do not maime,
And simply they shimmer,
Simmer, boil to bake the cakes,
For cakes and ale,
Activise or activate,
It's Adam's apple or buoyancy.

117
Pizzeria

No pizzeria for stealthy looks,
Though veritable at times,
Like a smeaking snake,
Can sink in a serpentine,
And a smooth gasket can do,
Well known spear of a girl friend,
Hair-do can settle the matter,
Or a friendly relationship.

Seamy dreams are too many,
Nabbing in a pavement indeed,
Like a ballarina does about,
Walking, stalking or cracking,
A marvellous joke for pith,
Or at the Editr's bench,
How smooth are the noble hands,
And a palm-tree grows atop,
Or a kinly palm at the most.

118
Throng

No snarling when gnarlad,
The tree is felled almost,
Like poseidon lost the eye sight,
Across the watery way a bier,
Yet smart is the smirch,
And God leaves us in lunch,
As in a pedagogic throng,
The victim falls to the victor.

Uncle has a carbuncle,
A meandering menace,
Like uncle Podger or cabin,
Tomfoolery of no Tom Sawyer,
Heckling for smacking or so,
We sing a bullaby,
To dull the sinners,
And for virtuosos,
Top secret is the throng.

119
The World

I must give way to no despair,
A connoisseur is not mild,
Like Friar Lawrence,
And the dreamy girls are few,
Or Juliet can be no chance,
No anger is in foresight,
And a clamour is for glamour,
Charm and grace stolted,
A menagerie is for no alms.

Gradation as regimen,
Like Dhoot Paperwar once,
The world was nice long ago,
For nagging and ragging,
Longevity extended the time,
Though a fiasco is calm,
The belligerent failure,
Upsets the human mind.

120
Mental Sickness

Darmouse not mentally sick is,
It's the human being,
Like carniving cognition,
May be carved sickness ascender,
Astute minds too bhunder,
To tend or to tender gifts,
For a taker or maker,
To seize the catch up.

Appetite as lamination,
Not cannibalistic attempt,
Like a severe punishment,
Jingoism is for Bumbledom,
A magazine for a rift to shoot out,
Slavish carnivals,
Only for uppoh menu,
Festivals can also peeve,
Grieve, mew or sew.

121
Reprisals

Azure is the sky endless,
We do not know the clue,
Like a plig for a gig,
As a gift of God,
A pizzaria on an eatout,
Edible oils are rich,
Frenzy clumsy soft,
Tasty foods are for foodies.

A lizard can check the roll,
Soul, mole, pole and toll,
Like padestrians overcowed,
Or a turnpike openwide,
No retaliation hence forth,
Thence forth and forthwith,
Commenced causive,
Paradigm is complex,
That carries inflections.

122
Conflicts

Sifting, shifting and drifting,
The conflicts play havoc,
Like the Beatrics and Hippies,
Prejudiced monuments,
Or hefty prodigious pondering,
Bell fry or tongue tyed tapering,
Which is to ringout and sing in,
Banging blang monstrous.

Pampering is no good anyway,
Imposters are forever happy,
Like the joblers jib akin,
Armless man is formless,
Amputated missile fondling,
Unbalanced replica,
Burning on a funeral pyre,
Or shooting out for God's help,
To cryout for Solon's philosophy.

123
Accolade

Troubadous are fine,
For they have accolades,
No trite in them so far,
No trousseux can trumpthems,
Like a death (circle) encircling,
Some troy indeed sole!
Paved are the caves,
As in shelleyan symbols.

Quietus for quietude,
An endless silence fetching,
Like a wretch bedumbed,
A numberless shadowed,
Squeezing or tearing,
As in Bangladesh war,
Tikkakan new complained,
Attitude as amplitude,
History reveals the standards.

124
Plagiarism

"Augurers say they know not",
Asps perhaps know better,
Or even charmful charmion,
Like a courteran, a courtier,
Octavo records well,
Rather a chronicles asleep,
Ferrid is the valuable egoist,
As in a thumping majority.

Effective copious abundant,
To cope with skull and will power,
Like an ailment set right,
Can be a hyacinthfully used,
For contour building delimitation,
Sometime nothing in cyber space,
Quest is for behest,
And the young world projects,
To denounce or announce.

125
Appreciation

A halo is built up magnanimous,
For some appeasement minimal,
Like sporadic events cluster,
Deadlock still mystifies the mint,
A treanuetrove, a treasurehunt,
No Mcnas gold yet please,
Biogas can build up the pageant,
Invented domicile dogged.

Loyalties questioned,
Destitutes too cry for fame,
Like fobs innumerable,
As latticed lattitudes,
The globe is oval surrounding,
If men are emarculated,
Eunuchs can prosper,
Eureka! Eureka!! is the end,
For penisy's children.

126
Catcalls

Catcalls do wonders to save us,
A native bench or inglespace,
Like the man made insularity,
Or circumnavigation round about,
Condescending the truth,
Boundless bondage battering,
Shattered after spotted,
Threatening monsters dote.

The spoils can result in,
To brush up the cockroaches,
Like the single bed-fellows,
Misappropriation can do a little,
And kingfishers or magpies throttle,
The eventful eerie enterprise,
Wallowing and swallowing,
Ditties we too shall write,
And look for the mystery beyond.

127
Bongo

Tango or bongo,
The world follows now,
Like a barge poised!
The sole remedy pocketed,
No hell of noise disturbs,
As sophistry banished,
Or a vanished volubility,
Some behavioural science.

Lukewarm reception,
To pheasants and peasants,
Like peacock, weeping,
Stricism as a virtue,
Haughty fellows surrender,
To ditty songs and nudes,
Virtuous is the aesthetics,
Thick skinned oberons,
And Titanias are joculex.

128
Delusion

Karaikol and caracksol,
Delude or collude,
Like the awesome illusions,
A vestigial prestige alludes,
May be a collision of fancies,
Or a smothering flower,
As flora and fauna,
The bisons can bear the truth.

If shaggy hair can wager,
Wave or weave the way out,
Like a balance upside down,
Catapulted in enormous way,
Empathy becomes sympathy,
Human race cheats others,
Animal kingdom strartles,
The imps and the pimps,
No matter for the tempo.

129
Accordance

Single handed protects,
Bellaros bellows again,
Like something awry goes,
Prochivities differ encore,
May be an oyster time,
Foetus is killed aghast,
Cruel and ferocious,
Speedy sulking too slow,
Filled with ironic fever.

Favour, fear striking aloud,
Like deceitful fraud,
Exploitation encumbers all,
Declared classification fending,
Mending and defending,
As in a flow of strong words,
Age old contravention,
A probable transcendence.

130
Sculptures

Sculptures can frame strictures,
Or opposing vendetta,
Like agony doubtful,
Apparent ambiguity,
A way for Doubting thamases,
Meretricious, mendacious,
Stupendous, defending,
For their own sustenance.

Stultification for solace,
And desparate disdain,
Like stratification open,
Marrifestation is the end,
As in a literary jargon,
Manifold revelations relative,
Terms indicate to vindicate,
Spiteful spiritual unrest,
Konpara deserves to be a temple.

131
Vanguard

No partisan outlook for vanguard,
When at once advances farther,
Like a homeguard front,
Multitudinous altitude,
For trekking or peeking,
Over lordship that betakes,
Human beings are dirty,
Meant for diaspora.

Keyhole morals or secrets,
Never tender resignations,
Like designations dictating,
Strange is the universe,
Ambush murders deployed,
Perpetuating as forest brigades,
Regionation of strength,
Inhuman wretchedness,
Wickedness as tirade.

132
Diaspora

Scandalous scams for bear,
For swear scaling matadors,
Bullfighters, camel riders,
Jackeys for sheep skins,
Like woolsacks of Lord Chancellors,
Eschequers invite incite,
The alien blood for *shikar*,
No longer simple alignment.

Secular estrangement as espoinage,
May flower goes on voyage,
Like an exemplary *fatwa*,
Declares to declaim,
As nascent encounter,
A niche is not cleavage,
Timidity tutors the tutclage,
Suffrage for adulthood,
Is in the green house.

133
Parvati

A para sonic dasher,
A pan sonic haber dasher,
A deva dasi, Shiva dasi,
Concubine to the Lord,
Like a paramilitary force,
That engulfs the parody,
Unless the conflict of ideas,
Rule the roost mostly.

Trial and error is no more,
Like eerie occult rapid force,
Enforcement of no property tax,
Or no man's land, zero hour,
"Ambition is madman's virtue",
Parvati is a beautiful damecuse,
Useful, innocent, pious, fraudulent,
At last to the coral strand,
Sumitra is also the same.

134
Hostility

Samples as amples,
Are for polio drops,
Like the drugs are stored,
To avert the adages,
A preserved Bordeaux wine,
The sinal column though strong,
Yet yields to hostility,
An embargo latent.

Like the hostage taken,
Venus protects the madrigals,
Or disembankation,
Nastalgia avered,
Self poise as nausia,
Distinguishes extinction,
A domain as main of bay,
But no baying please,
So hostile is the world.

135
Guest House

Don't coax a fox,
He will hoax you et al,
Like a howling wind,
Or a burrowing badger,
Ferrets are many,
Ample in the guest house,
Or an euphora of strangers,
The world remains calm.

A duplex fort as edifice,
My mind fluctuates,
Like a new direction vetting,
Caesar is awake, let him so,
No haena is alive for a long,
New Gods, old guards are aplenty,
I can't shed crocodile tears,
Though pears and spears are keen,
One more over is over.

136
Blood Speaks

Blood speaks and squeaks,
Of the chicken hearted chics,
Like the spear heading lancers,
My emblem is cataract,
A logo shorter compressed,
For entertainment,
Or spying selfish ends.

So so in the courtesy to swear,
Timbrels are gambols,
Or meandering repulsions,
Like a vow or Wow or so!
No more disease to undermine,
Squeezing the sugarcane juice,
Chimua is cruel,
Or mephistopheles of Faustus,
I regret but segregate,
Empedocles on Eatna.

137
Festoons

Restive are the festoons,
Cartoons and spartanns,
No menelaus, no Paris now,
Like the forgotten history,
We need the lion's share or so,
No cannibals but beautification,
Regional religiveity confess,
As cash in pay up old custom.

Not many devils are active,
Though for a satirical aim,
Like poetic diction mollifies,
Emulated sarcase,
Euphimism to please,
Sadism to masochism,
Surrealism is active,
Too many are Hindu festivals,
But they are festivities of KONPARA.

138
In the Sky

I found Konpara but once,
Like a flash of light in the sky,
Gorgons damaged the devils,
Of less statue mature,
Or selicm at times,
At large a comet, a meteor,
May be sedetory simple,
As a fine garment.

I call it Humboldt gift,
Like pizza ignored for a long,
A quiet showdown but rapacious,
Embryo as in a womb,
An unknown figure far off,
Metanamy as eviction,
Ejaculation endeared to us,
Some Freudian concept,
Or secret solipsism as true.

139
Raconteurs

I can tell stories as novelties,
If I read out I can lead,
Like a master of arts,
The livid as the intrepid,
Acting and reacting,
A confluence to influence,
They prepare and cajole,
Some men are far great.

No hot-bed but hotpot,
Caught as hot blooded by all,
Like poverty stricken worst,
And a theme forecasts the fame,
A combat for renown all that,
Proceedings decide the pre-eminence,
Jettisoned as on the Mississippi,
With laconic arguments,
We also enjoy ourselves.

140
Widowhood

Nefarcious widowhood is a thrift,
A parsimony on parchment,
Like a written document,
With none as a protector,
Wrinkles capture sooner,
Or later, a campfire, a bonfire,
And swinging foliage,
Repatriate the recollections.

Young widows are better,
For a new betrothal,
Like palfreys can succumb,
Or bear the weight as brunt,
Front, stunt and morale,
Telephonic talks are common,
For afiance no defiance,
As angry moods offend,
Defend and also confound.

141
Force

"Hardly hedge rows",
Perhaps a beacon light as seashore,
Fulbright scholarships,
Lit amalgamation acclaimed,
No pause is for force, power,
Manpower, sparsely sequence,
Peaceful face an angst,
The world is light altogether.

Vials and phials rebound,
Industrious goodness,
Like aimful disciplined tryst,
Needful coronation complacent,
Denonment cultivates the crisis,
Cosy phase as fanciful
Newness is arduous musical
Stature as a feature,
Can speak values out.

142
The Seer

Fervently fervid as fervour,
Favour for a fiancee,
Love clicks, luck clicks,
Like one gluck to grow,
Fidgeting ruses so many,
We might live for others,
Sympathy mercy fussy,
Pegasun can't fly then.

But Hippocrene to flow,
Peering the seer does,
Previews and reviews,
Are pee wits at present,
Prudence is for self,
Perf or big gulf,
Trust in the breast,
Fast is the heart,
And felicitation.

143
In the Fray

In the fray for an array,
A natural aplomb nice,
Like the quarrelsome mice,
Twice blessed or even thrice,
Engagement for dating,
Doting, coating and looting,
Dowry deaths as manifold,
Fleece the button hole.

An obscurantist succinet,
Salacious, jagacious,
Like the truthful none,
Veering to care for a more,
A barmaid in a pub,
Liviatham in a tub,
A cub is a better rub,
Falsifying falsehood,
"And the echo rings".

144
Mature Nature

Mature Nature as forefront,
Plays havoc with fate,
Like Heavenly grace, trace,
Face, brace, charm and form,
Defaulters fear and tear,
Odyssey is for their rescue,
As honoured reverence,
Achilles heel is ahead.

An argosy for melancholy,
Archids can do wonders,
Like alms arid for aria,
Wonderful climate for aberrations,
As amnesia overpowering,
Dimentia cando its worst,
Some messiah can teach,
And preach us lovely,
When the gloom dies out.

145
Dacoits

Dacoits pray to Devi, Kali Mata,
And Goddess of love or muse,
Like Venus of KONPARA,
For a mandatory doggerel,
No blackmailing for steria is sweet,
A natural sweetmeat,
They might not believe,
As nectar in the sieve.

Staunch deliberations hangup,
And severe punishment,
Like storage relieved,
As solemnity long lost,
Sine curers stand still,
As in a stand off the nill,
No bargaining at all,
Goddess might save them,
While tendered apologies.

146
Nature Tempts

Nature is for high stature,
Tantalising, tiltillating,
Scintillating, tottering,
Like a sweet delicacy,
A blaring chante cleer,
That crows, trows, honks,
A showpiece enormous,
Costly fastfood unusual.

Lavishly ravishing luxuriant,
No stigma leaves on the priest hood,
Like a laburnum grove,
With a sceptical labyrinth,
No chronicle holds a record,
As in a paved way pedestal,
For some jovial company as it is,
Snout is for a bout,
And she ports for others.

147
Heroines

In this land only heroines,
And mysogenic heroes are there,
Like missogarnist leaders,
Frontrunners, forerunners,
To foreshadow, overshadow,
Haunt the hall mark,
No wickedness sustains,
Nor chickenery persists.

If they desist they dither also,
Like a boiling samovan,
Determine or deride to deter,
Avatars of cosmogarry,
Prudes as lonely nudes,
Restless spinsters, shrews,
Warring ventilators,
Weathercocks venerable,
Shadowy vampires.

148
Energy

Energy entails to clench,
A boas constrict or cobre dance,
Like a garlanded Venus,
Konpara is climatic—
A beautiful woman upset,
Restless, sighing, fidgeting,
As if life were over,
In simple fortitude.

Adroitness stead fast,
Like a drifting nature,
Can gather no mess energy,
A momentum as such,
It's an end by itself,
Simple apathy avers, averts,
Advertises, specifies,
An upset factor,
More or less kinetic.

149
Consummation

No ennui in these columns,
Consummation is fool proof,
Like the relative density,
Bosh! "It's paltry to be caesar",
"... a parcel of their fortune",
"Now Brutus will speak,
Mighty Brutus",
Consummate objective correlates.

Clinch the matter forever,
To corroborate or elaborate,
Like the concern of happy birds,
A dredging machine, a beacon light,
A skylark in the skull,
Perhaps a skillful dungeon,
Has onus though gibberish,
Slimy jaws are perfect,
Climax is the end.

150
Stockade

Stockade is as blockade,
Ordained by ordenance,
Estranged easement,
Like the fear forgotten,
Indian impasse,
A staunch compass,
Can lash, smash, rash,
As in a fashion parade.

Blasphemous, engraving,
No pessimistic outlook,
Like ingredients encashed,
Falconny is a free/will,
Spokespersons are too many,
Memsahibs unveiled,
Mementos marred,
For subsequent truth,
Imprison the froth.

151
Adam and Eve

Phenomenon to phenomena,
Single to dual to plural,
Two fold to manifold,
Lie the manifold paper,
They increase the folks,
Not salacious alone,
But pugnacious also,
No longer seclusions.

Cadavers are too many,
Like the mushroom growth,
In a quadruplicate season,
They grew and perished,
Manuscripts implead,
Plead and lead high,
Illusory linguistic galore,
No one is some of creation,
Yet it is desideratum.

152
Plethora of Events

As a plethora of events,
No conscience forbears,
Like that forwears,
His majesty forbids,
A ripped symbiosis,
Angry maladies,
Never help the men,
Fanfare is there.

Sarascenic architecture,
That portends some mixed art,
Like an original brainstorm,
Ample is the sample,
Marvels no smutty rap,
Series of taunts or blows,
Pavillion is the top trick,
Mature as well as age,
State, rage, wage.

153
Love and Heart

Smart heart as in love,
Heart and sex can't by dry,
Like fry being wry,
Whopping without sops,
(Yet no blatant lie),
A fish can also gush,
Lover try and fail,
As meeting eyes.

Something crooning to show,
Guady giddy teddy bears,
Of mowing movements slow,
Like a heart felt condolence,
Or a literary defence,
Counter offence, no offence,
Seizing the crazy eyes,
Eye to eye, no eye-sore,
Can stop the guise forever.

154
Indian Mules

Packmules, lumber jacks,
Make India great,
Their fate absolute at Konpara,
Like absolutism honoured,
Deposition, imposition,
Inbued or combined,
Fairness in all,
As sincerity great.

Oh! how old I am,
Depressed compression,
For suppression manifold,
Like impressive impressarios,
"Readyness in all",
For goodness and death,
No letter to Heaven,
God is very far off,
Vagueness an baroqueant.

155
Celerity

As a speed of movement active,
Paper tigers for rubber bullets,
Like an endemic mortality,
Gangsterism is sporadic,
Newness as business like,
Ancestrial property disposed off,
Vendor and vendee quarrel,
As in for bread in bakery.

Aeronautical husbandry,
Peek or shriek you are a man,
Like a melodious song,
And a song bird flirts,
Formidable mindset speaks,
Creaks it is not meck,
Idioms are endemic,
As in a borrowed wealth,
Or even a borrowed health.

156
Confutations

Most cunning and stunning,
Computations live for imputations,
Like in a wonder land,
Alice or chalice lives for others,
Exorbitant rates chagrined,
As for philosophic confusius,
No more frowning or crowning,
Salamance was great.

As daring predominance,
A cut off or cut out,
Like drop outs lingering,
Accost the costly rhythm,
And a frowning browning,
Can write no prose poem,
Some knowledge is let off,
Or let out on a layout,
May be a bright thermos.

157
Electronic Media

A pulse for pubration,
Sensation with no fabrication,
Like a medivere medium,
No longer for scheduled module,
Dirty body prevails,
Avails a panoply,
Again a seimitor,
A daggar sharp whetted.

An oxymoron panoramic,
Inundates the flow further,
Like a cupola unknown,
Uncovered and discovered,
A nudity of the secrets,
Thrilling as a mass murder,
Or probable fiesta,
Nor in Rotten Buroughts,
Counties are plentiful.

158
Dog-days

As dogged days are dog days,
The heat is over of dubbed youth,
Like the nonsense poetry,
As pounced or announced,
Abetters and abettoires,
Are early approvers no culprits,
Seldom bite the dogs,
Dogs in the manger.

Fresh selfish fishes,
As in Dolphin's nose,
Like preming young lads,
Deltrone and embark,
An anchorage of prawns,
Meaningless obscurantism,
No absorption further,
A proxy gull innocent,
Is a white sea gull now.

159
Replica

Enforcement, a skill,
Spoinage poised a little,
Like a fine sincere,
Entumbed in the burial,
No jeer, no sneer now,
And the brutal elements,
Can't be beefed up,
And beefeaten take care.

Beelzebn next to Satan,
Can't evince clemency,
Like a shipwrecked sailor,
That is a revengeful soldier,
Monsters aren't in ulster,
As in the smart upstart,
No downtrodden sirens,
As simple scumples,
Egoistic egotism bursts out.

160
Sequence

Sequence in social consequence,
Spill over spills the beans,
Like a darting danger,
As in a senecan drama,
Perhaps denouncement,
As embroidered gossamer,
Flimsy fragment or figment,
That springs out and rings.

Neither fart nor harty,
In battlements new,
Like pragmatic dogmas,
Silent sardiner afar,
Imago of imagery,
Combatants battling,
One battens for the other,
As in a rare square,
When stones are costly.

161
Sublimation

No sordid boon of bonfire,
As in a supire posture,
Let us not be all asleep,
Chicory chicanery,
And "Coffee House Policions",
Like good riddance,
Conglomerate religion,
Simply sniks and dies out.

A wangling wanker,
Disturbs the peace,
Like a ritualist unusual,
To sup or to supplant,
Man is to implant,
And never to complain,
A wonderland suffocating,
A bonafide risk,
No frigidity once for all.

162
A Poem Indeed

A midriff for cardiff,
A subaltern, a midship,
Like a businessman central,
Safe in the supremo,
As in egalitarian,
A contrivance indeed,
Intellectual property,
Some goody goody eyes.

"Ribboned to stick in his coat",
An artist, a fatalist,
Like Sardello or Saul Bellow,
Fortune favours not all,
A celebrity with a crevice,
Follows the fame,
For its own sake shallow,
Hollow, for a halo!
As a truncated poem.

163
A Sacrificial Lamb

Sanctified as a lamb,
Escapes the sordidness infact,
Like a deed exemplified,
Some frontispiece,
Latchets, satchets as well,
Like keyhole morals,
Morale demands,
The mural frescoes.

To outsource the incomer,
Or at least the insider,
Like a spinning top,
We solicit harmony,
Sadistic tendency,
And the camouflage persists,
Indians die for God,
They live for themselves,
Lambs, kids, chaffs, heifers.

164
Proselytizers

A land of proselytizers,
A faith single is rare,
Like an ironic method,
For sordani achievement,
Sinister faces monstrous,
In a mango grove, coconut glade,
Some shade and light,
The deer and snakes can do.

An impressive thumb impression,
Imprecates a lot,
Like incursions tended,
No sebrism while I speak,
For my speech is for reforms,
Reformation is an inborn,
Quality not prescribed,
Or a balanced stage,
No impediment at all.

165
Spouse

"... this espoused Saint",
Not Mary Powel,
Like C. Woodcock short life,
A metaphysical mortal,
Lives and dies for cognition,
A poetic saint scholarly,
Ignores Chitra Lekha,
Amrapali and Umrao.

Puzzled or whistled,
It's for gazelle eyes,
Like a deer peeks,
With a peeping comedy,
Enveloped in love,
An applause a chance,
For some gratification,
No catastrophe more so,
Furthermore a sugar candy.

166
Spoon Feeding

"Do this or this, or else we damn thee",
No response yet,
As in Kubla Khan, ethnic norms,
Like an estranged significance,
A display of some strange land,
Some penchant splendour,
Blended with no blemishes,
As in a *Katari* of bandits.

No credulous beatification,
No faithful canonization,
Like Marabar caves deeply wide,
Celestral revels as revelation,
The star at eventide in Venus,
Stupified or pacified,
Let usn't bother or smother,
Of no vindicative indication,
A spurious decoration.

167
Nescience

Tight nude fight as a rite,
In Konpara, Chandragutti,
They worship Venus,
Or Vaishno Devi a Goddess,
Like adverse perverse tone,
And thus propitiate Gods,
A rip van winkle strange,
Unknown to the feeble fame.

"O with end in the garland of war",
A feasible faze of life,
Like proserpina enfolded,
Bushy tails or pig tails,
And tailoring streaming,
Seamstresses sewing a new,
Garments decorate the dictation,
Life is in the stone,
Sculpture, sepulture.

168
Stiles

Philanthropic determinism,
Destitutes the devilry,
Peer Harbour or Diego Garcia,
Like a proof of perambulafs,
God's children sight,
But not in Konpara so much,
To go amuck among the pandals,
Stiles are still stout—hard bound.

Ulterior motives of Gods,
Estrange Venus or devotees,
Like schematic schism,
Trusted or encrusted,
Man is great, too big,
No madrigal is enough to applaud,
Undermined or drudged look,
Skirting the animosity,
Stupified, mystified.

169
Dungeons

Sensitive souls show the trends,
For they are nuisant at times,
Like a scare crow browbeating,
Cuisine is all right often,
A culdesac for nutrients,
Or a doctor's dieting for health,
And the patient's wealth gone,
Drugs are no doubt bugbears.

Soul's tragedy is all right,
Simplified drudgery,
Like a lost figure alone,
Mortified, stultified, testified,
Of course, everyone is safe,
Venus protects one and all,
More so the dead devotees,
Or even the necropheles,
Incertain dungeons.

170
Burglers

No burglers are in India,
No thieves at all gentle,
Like a think tank quoted,
Insolence a dogged word,
Of meretricious trinkets,
Wretcher seen in Konpara,
May not be Indian,
Pity that not to identify them.

For selection and erections,
Rabbits are a better choice,
Not to play true as the monsoon,
Like age old defaulters can,
The glory of warfare or Siachen,
Jhelum is the best river,
For riveries and cosmetics,
Simplify the truth cognizent,
Aho! sit on a sedan chair.

171
Delicacies

Sedulous, credulous, fabulous,
Like comets in a starry world,
Lugubrious fathen are dismal,
And the inevitable, horizontal,
Never grows to heaven,
I am in the mortal world,
Of paeans and madrigals,
As plenty of goblets.

Rectified but bereft,
Yet globules are offered,
Like the carots to weigh,
Fashion parades peeve,
Sieve and also greave,
Dimmed or deemed delicacy,
Lolling or falling,
It's a reverend custom,
To eat or not to eat.

172
Saplings

Like meticulous melee,
Thronging long as butchery,
No redemption yet for the Goddess,
Benumbed is Venus,
And Konpara as Komintang,
Lives and lines up a long way,
A lea of fleas or glee,
"No more by thee my steps shall be".

Far away, far away,
To the distant lands we go,
Like flavour savoury,
We are on the trak but slack,
A sustaining disposed off case,
It's but seeping and seething,
May be a cucurbit family,
Veggies are big now simple,
Sampling as saplings.

173
Bathos

Timid fellows for livid gallows,
Liquidation or litigation,
Like spill over all the rest,
Might be we all goal keepers,
Not for kowtowing at all,
And spree is free,
Though sandwitched we are,
We are good for stratagems.

Fraternal feelings focus,
For eternal emblematic symbols,
Dakshayani a Godly Goddess,
Renamed a Katyayani,
Like Venus as Herperus,
Versifiers sings to glorify,
As unscheduled mythos,
Never gives way to bathos,
Denial is the strength.

174
Cherryblossoms

Past mystery is fart afoot,
Ghastly mystery is nasty,
Like a short sighted view,
Spurting firth, gushing forth,
Embezzlement at the end,
Fazes the maze,
Bondage perturbs or disturbs,
Or at the most dissipates.

Occasional pejorative purpose,
A dandelion can grow nautch,
Like the gridle overblown,
And a blowing wind restless,
Grows no peace anywhere,
Ladybird! Ladybird!!
Grant us not duodecimo,
For our own interests,
And cherry blossoms too!

175
Venus

Wild or mild we are beguiled,
Song birds are single,
If they can't duets,
"... farthest He brides",
Like flying off to its resort,
Her rendezevous is unknown,
We know not God sends them,
Or Venus of Konpara.

Detrimental delicious,
As in Elysian Mountains,
She brings an Elixir,
Like exhaustion removed,
Contagion is confirmely,
Aparthied do not know,
As in Kimberly mines,
Diamond is an emerald,
A beautiful stone culture.

176
Variety

Variety in double singleness,
Lovelorn eyes speak out,
Like a silent voice mirthful,
Tired is the mire of squire,
Anchored in a vast lake,
No crocodile but water hyacinth,
Complex personage,
Still the persona is great.

"The heaven above and road belasme",
No pressure for the wordly life,
Like the ferns grazed up,
Fine to be acclamatization,
Grape fruit is a big one,
And grapes are sweet or sour,
Mildred isn't come so far,
Moistened goitre,
Creates also some oedema.

177
Relationships

Bellicose camels of Bedoi tribes,
Evolve belligerent relationships,
Like mercy forgotten,
A branch of olive sustains,
Polite, impolite, volatile,
Play the latent mischief,
Rather a deserted look out,
To fight on the camped camels.

Feedback deemed fit,
Set back sermonised,
Like a "blithe new comer",
Baseless are the imputations,
Writhing seribes synchronise,
Remaining relationships restore,
"Fitful fever" frowns often,
Ah! lantern symbolic,
Celestial duties wonderous.

178
Thuggy

Thuggy and buggy were common,
In ancient India, Konpara,
Scintillating Secunderabad,
Sarsaparilla, sticky,
Like ducats hoarded,
And, on run away with,
Loot arson psychosomatism,
And now and then psychosis.

Pilgrims adored or adorned,
No brotherhood of sisters,
Like mentors and centaurs,
Everywhere Aginicount,
Or even poitiers,
Venus dictates terms now,
So as to rise or fall,
The fall is over,
The Spring is ahead.

179
Pelicans

A little pelicans as Dominicans,
Monks or skunks a fear,
Like spiritual guidance,
Adumbrating now and then,
So as to rank and file,
Conscious of the status,
Slimy, flimsy, filmy,
Pelicans have no jaws.

Fanfare, software,
Hardware is nowhere,
Sombambulists sing softly,
Crooning, shooing to clamber,
Ah! chamber of commerce,
As in Konpara stuffy stalking,
No stocking for canons,
Leave aside the picture,
Like new Gods and Goddesses.

180
At Large

Damon and Pythos,
Gorgon slays the dragon,
Like an atonement,
Delayed pansies sow fancies,
An atmospheric pressure,
Sissies are fussy,
Clumsy Goddess grows,
Cynderella syndrome.

No Parvati, no Sumitra,
No Venus, no Andromecha,
Like a deluge inundated,
Only a tombstone remembers,
An epitaph hardly remains,
"Whole life was spent in waters",
Am I so, God is great,
I pray to him day and night,
A man of action at large.

181
Constriction

Some incest in the fest too,
A test in Venus and Cupid,
Hesperus, Amora Damogorgo,
Like a fussy tumult,
Rhetoric emblematic,
Persona as the epitome,
All but nonsense, absurd,
Simple adsorption perhaps,,
Bubtchers for bitches.

As in Indian schedule,
Like module unearthed,
No disappointment further,
A disarm or a tug of war,
Rather a merry-go-round,
Or elso sputnic idealism,
No Doda district to constrict,
But rockets fall on innocence.

182
Compositions

Man is the worst enemy of God,
No canopy, no panoply,
No Indian hates others,
Like a Dernogorgen for death,
Dreaming the conundrums,
Sumptuous skills skin us,
Tan or ban or fan the creeks,
Lavish is the languish.

Mean Muslims are not too many,
Lepakshi is a proof as Sphinx,
Indians are not quaint,
Though gossamers they are,
A quaint master key holds,
Many a lock or shock,
And the quirk can shirk,
Not masseurs are alike,
Selfimposed compositions.

183
Marshylands

A tab for tabulations, capitulation,
Copulation or master monsters,
Like a man of meanness,
Or a Master of ceremonies,
A miraculous minx,
Venus protects and defends,
But the mischievous boys,
Ogle or boggle with circe.

Baptists can save them,
From a meandering run off,
A winsome wino is there,
Like the cell biology,
Or even prognostication,
Masterminded the gifts,
Wildfire as a pageant,
Will-o-the wism moves about,
At night at marshy lands.

184
Wildfire

Venus brings no wild fire,
Three Goddesses can do it,
A burning fire of Aphrodite,
Amorous, amoral,
Like solicitude anxious,
Unfulfilled rummage,
Frescoes are many in Ajanta,
Manoeuvring all that.

Like destitution deplored,
Abnegation is necessary for self,
As amazed empiricism,
Gusto of the furtion,
Of turgid language,
Museology and metrology,
Likelihood outbreaks,
And attached detachment,
Sovereignty rules the serenity.

185
Diatribe

We hold placards highly,
Not blackguards at least,
Like blackheads on the skin,
Or sinful Konpara tidy,
Winchester can deal with it,
Perhaps digital blackmail,
And sometime diatribe,
With political vendetta.

Can we dump the stump at rumpters,
We would if we could,
Like wincing commencement,
"Drudgery of the desk",
As exhausted exertion,
Scenario of windmills, Sanchopanzar,
Cutlery vetting avowal,
For ecstatic avoidence,
Farther exigent diatribe.

186
Seapula

"... The noise of battle rolled",
Excaliber was never seen again,
King Arther was no more head,
Like a wounded soldier gone,
And the scapula was broken,
Konpara the round table up,
A close down for goodness,
Lost circumstances of greenery.

Sir Orfeo has left,
Evridice was lovely,
Like Venus who is old,
Life is for evangelism,
"Fearful trip is done",
"Now grim and desolate",
"Obscurest night involves the sky",
I can sing a fathomless song,
A magpie is soft however.

187
Muddle

Like mastubatory fancies,
Indians practise goodness,
As in a fantasy native world,
"Death closes all",
Though wankers never wank,
Yet they can wangle,
Wrangle, spangled tangle,
May be God's will like.

The muddle as a riddle,
No Indian loves Molech,
Like a straight forward hero,
Saddled with sanguine glory,
A salvo swaddled supreme,
Swagger with daggers,
Baggy, shaggy and wanton,
Riggish maidens do not tire,
For their attires scuffle.

188
Secret

"Death after life is sweet",
A rent shall decide to scuttle,
Like a network is betwork,
Cattle cannot prattle,
Mavericks know better,
To unseat the Goddess,
Docile deities demur not,
Friendly fondness fondles.

Mares and wares fare not well,
Jump the gun recalcitrant,
Like a citadel protected,
As usual we defend it,
Pre-eminence as a concert,
Search for research,
A *Kundalini* force, vortex,
The Goddess is all in all,
I believe all eminence.

189
Pre-eminence

All above others as it is,
Oodles for beadles or oof,
Like "Blind Fury comes with Abhored shears",
No vaccnity but proximity,
Theatrical movements align,
Armaments disarmaments,
Goes with prolixity.

Horrified as pre-eminent,
As structural incarceration,
Like behaving perfection,
Theoretical superiority,
And malafide benevolence,
Service to disservice,
Prominence declines,
Expensive exaggeration,
Structural bathes,
That enervates atlast.

190
Toddlers

Badgers and bandicoots,
Justify and testify,
To officiate official, officious,
Duties and motives,
Like the ultra vives constitution,
Institutions restitute,
The burning scuttle of coals,
Toddlers also doddle or cuddle.

Drenching exhaustion,
Tweedle-dum tweedle-dee,
Like an extravagant buzz,
Some slogan to mislead,
And gossip as radiance,
Dominading predominance,
Elixir is a turf,
Crooming or frowning,
We look for a little hope.

191
Tughlak

Cho in Chennai,
Macaroni or music in pizzara,
Eat out as eatery,
Like the lame and the blind,
From Dilli to Daulatabad,
No crooks, nor creeks,
Toddlers as fondling,
Breast feeding breaks in.

Profligacy as legacy,
Stench stinks with kinks,
Like genomes add up to genes,
Nothing is common,
At times we live for others,
History is a grand proof,
Proficiency of a chairperson,
Persists to insist,
Modernity maims me.

192
Denoument

Fluent and confluent,
Things stand aloof,
Like barbaric assiduity,
Though baffling cockatrice,
Is nice for the day to say,
Dragon fly is better flying,
Though can't fly billiards,
Still soccer is nice.

Barbaric infiltration,
Flutter and flurry the best food,
Like a stinking stench,
A drastic nuisance,
A trite argument as environs,
Recalcitrant refuse,
As in a dramatic revue,
Supposition is brief,
Opposition is strong.

193
A Wardrobe

A wardrobe can ward off,
The spiritual beauty,
Like abulting seritures,
Woman needs man, man feeds woman,
As in a wardrobe wonderful,
Alarmingly graceful,
Schizophrenia major malady,
Garners with some speeches.

Acadamic necessities,
Freeze the golden fleece,
Off seasons are on and on,
Like affluent influence,
But no savagery anywhere,
The monsoon has just set in,
We are the scape goats,
And the mosquito menace,
Can ravage us all.

194
Burrows

When you dither you also deter,
While deterioration is strong,
Like deferment dangerous,
Aderanged psychopath,
Can do little for fellowmen,
Uncouth ravenous ravens,
Although rugged they are,
With occasional civilities.

Konpara is a cultured land,
No effluents nor pullutants,
Like a landmark recorded,
Drilling mills are common,
As unfounded burrows,
Stealthy folks are still good,
Sorrows never spill out,
Man is a pious animal,
And a chaste woman too.

195
Scapegoats

Eating and bleating,
As common perspectives,
Like sinking boats boom,
No more they live active,
A beggonly life pursues,
And seasons are severe,
To make them host,
Owls can never do it.

Rags and ragtime enrage us,
Like of spend thrift nature,
Bills and wills protract,
Life time languor,
Can't be candid,
As in an endemic thrift,
Nature is mature,
And statue can falsify,
Repugnance is mystical.

196
Bridge Course

Pambam bridge is falling,
Falling, falling and falling,
No Venus can save it,
Like inevitable loss total,
Sagging sins can sever,
Salient disservice simple,
Olive branch is fresh,
As a spruce twig.

Bridge coarse is delectable,
Sacred and savvy,
Like a simple small sojourn,
With a devan of arms,
And a sinful adulteress,
Sinks and dies,
In a hell of heaven,
Cavern is a tavern,
And a manmade delusion.

197
Severe Senility

Like severe senility simmering,
Deoderal ulcer grows,
No subsidied wealth grows,
It mows the truth,
Or the deadly pain persistent,
Panorama, cosmorama,
A peddlers caravan,
Or "O my daughter, O my daughter".

A sturgeon, cavior and roe,
Can make food tasteful,
Like a pickled egg of sperm,
Unless a row sows,
Madness fast growing,
A spousy misuse to cheat,
Beat or treat,
A sweetmeat can do much,
Life an extravaganza.

198
Enormous Trout

An elaborate enormous trout,
Like a fawning spawn,
A fay is in fairyland,
Not to decompose the body,
A saucy pause indeed,
Though a nauty nector,
Grand is the grandma's,
Fables, sable shroud.

A dim bedlamp,
Or bedlam beggars subtle,
(Like "thieves of time"),
Encounter is just for death,
Jig is although big,
And the western love smacks,
Spooks tells simple stories,
As in embroidered night,
When the village folk gather.

199
Nature's Own Climate

As in egocentric innocence,
We make marmalade,
Like Amul butter for better half,
As in a bethel,
A niche of pastor's climate,
No cleavage for a matron,
Or rather a patron saint,
As in a lullaby song.

Though scuttled in a chapel,
Or Aixla-chapel warfront,
Like the war lords accused,
Similar in the simple stunt,
Scenario of calf-love,
Cowboys as betters mostly,
Brand new love-knot,
Modern go back attitude,
No Kenilworth castle hence.

200
Freedom

Freedom brings in boredom,
(And no thraldom can veer),
When ventilation wears the wind,
Like an accolade denied,
As in Rann of Kutch or Bombay High,
Something is barren missed,
Booing a bow-vow theory,
Topsy turvy appreciation.

Mannipulative mannequins,
Skirmishes sheen or keen nacke,
Like the Pomerian dogs do,
With pomp, conceited deceit,
Though dogeared they are not,
Viscosity a modern technique,
Rather a patriotic fervour,
Frenetic fanatic fascimile,
Fantastic disposition.

201
Salvoes

"Death will come when it will come",
Pushpa speaks truth,
New versions for salvation,
Salvoes do for themselves,
Like Sacharine its duty,
As in San Salvador,
The death toll is high,
An earthquake measures the quake.

Postmortem proves the cause,
As in Jamaica in God sent,
Like punishment in store,
Sweat and blood procures,
No remorse for the dead,
At a time gun shorts desery,
Some unknown proven smear,
Best sold books are,
For God's praise alone.

202
Alms

As in an arms race in Konpara,
Alms fly about competively,
Like a fly over bridge,
As a way out or a way in,
Of sportive spirit in marathon,
They pose up the fray,
Armageddon a catastrophic end,
Against the injustice.

We prophecy God's arrival,
The hedge-row and bugbear,
Like the phenomena protected,
Sperecal numericals bogging,
Figures run into figureheads,
Small people beg,
Great personae donate,
No inimical end tends,
As in a downtown, the ghetto.

203
Repugnance

Besolted and besmirched,
Bete'noirs shipwrecked,
Like a small petty person,
We are original at least,
Palmistry is a fool proof,
Through a staunch disgust,
Reputation repugnant,
Polemical portal open.

No hedgehogs can disturb,
The hedonistic front,
Like a dent of disgrace,
"Fearful trip is done",
The proprietory is gone,
"Hear father hear the arm below",
The Russell Institute is enough,
To teach the taught,
Some salvo at the most.

204
Restaurant Culture

Penalty to venality,
And then to banatty,
Like a sordid boon,
"Mewhing and puking in nurses arms",
If we vend to live,
A sarcophagus all that lives,
Copycats for eat outs,
A restaurant culture.

Age old Aeschyles alive,
Though an unknown alien land,
Like samovar to scuffle,
We are united mankind,
Parleys and pagodas ponder,
Though fall prostrate,
Pageantry is salient anyhow,
Satirical testimony is,
For the purblind world.

205
Careerists

Prognostication to presage,
Visage or even garbage,
A pause with no cause,
Like the child labour ruled out,
Art is for artifice peeving,
Indian birds are prudes again,
Not malicious or salacious,
Threshold is sagacious.

No gout for a bout,
Gentle to refute the angels,
Like rebelous sprouting,
Mendicants are quacks,
Charon's cross, souls across,
Rivers styx, Lethe, Acheron,
Cerberus is awake,
Impostors are compost manure,
Tenure, censure, retired life.

206
Conflicts

Though annuled,
"All all are gone,
Old familiar faces",
Like garnered conflicts,
Virginity woos Indian soil,
Fertile sterile motile,
Fatal of doubtful motives,
As in historic faith.

In cultured Konpara,
Process is a recess for thesis,
Like deduction inducted,
No confrontation hypocrite,
Confident indulgence,
Preserved and secured,
Preference in torrential,
Drenched and stenched,
Yet it is strict occultism.

207
Lass

Lass is a boss now,
Like a mass as bass,
Measuring rod as thief,
No Venus but a Janus,
Doubled edged sword yet,
Perfect eminence simple,
We might feel or steal,
As mercuric volatile.

Permanent sibilant fuss,
Mind finds the kind,
A liege for the siege,
Like masterminded yoke,
Circumstantial evidence,
No profligate dump yet,
Biogas can settle the issues,
Fire flies have no fire within,
Though brittle they can glitter.

208

At Bay

Resembling the semblance of knapsark,
Lenient view taken for granted can sack,
Laccadaisical to hover and crack,
Like style or file put in stigma of rack,
Conventions, inventions also shrubes,
Appliances taken up create pet craft,
Astrophy or strophe in ode plumber,
An arrow remains a lofty sharp shaft,
And promptness perhaps paving the way,
As uncertainty that case mostly thump,
Of God any the orders cannot stay,
Sump annot limp and remains a himp,
Beauty shall be a sterile hope of ray,
That can keep an enemy off at bay.

209
Glitz

Flagged or ragged you are finely brisk,
Unrevealed is that an unknown text,
No more scampering as gnawing own risk,
Like an assembled showy shelf of pretext,
A learning or burning stealthy slip type,
A leader as if the question parrying,
When doom comes in slussing pursing as hype,
Purloming picaresque tarrying,
The forehead that we can for a long gaze,
We must feel since only health is a craze,
Pleasantry is a jovial joke to faze,
A new cob is with fresh tender maize,
An aerial attach primordial blitz,
And pinate penal pristine is the glitz.

210
Flight

Man at the threshold of life is lying,
Eventide so are even bitterly sighing,
Penguins and pelican must be dying,
Like the superstition somewhere frying,
At times picasso saves us for money,
None is at fault like a young colt,
In India we have enough money, honey,
No doubt it is purported blue from holt,
And a scholar may give you a taunt,
Strategy is a hiss or kiss like strap,
A shameful Brahmin convert cannot haunt,
Injurious rabidness can only wrap,
To absorption it is anyway clinging,
The matter is rinsed before wringing.

211
Sinister

Simple life is a receding pet loan,
Like the cleansed sample plan of a lee,
Landmark with no layout as a clay flown,
A discarded friend has not at all glee,
Alien style of living is good simple,
As a marvellous rapture of full plea,
A citizen a denizen pimple,
Moot speeches sizzle and assure no flea,
Wonder must baffle and surprise danger,
Among the leaders nobody can be mad,
Let us think God is never a stranger,
Be after the dates you a fad,
In a country anyone can minister,
If he fails too go to be sinister.

212

A Wooden Horse

Enemies cannot defeat but destroy,
With downcast eyes to God you may report,
A wooden horse is for invincible troy,
Glory and flora smell sweet and deport.
Like frozen phrases that also support,
Network and pet work can prattle persuade,
Eradition opposes a fraud rapport,
The seers peer and amply dissuade,
May be wish of stir suitable to fir,
No one wants to resemble noble cur,
Even if he is astin to a plain stir,
And a vien without a fresh single bur,
History cannot get rid of colourful bid,
Interminable bondage wringing a bid.

213
Tantan Race

Hagged or gagged to death in stable,
Sampled and trampled as the dapper wit,
Ragged or bagged is certain, a fable,
Like a lampoon that sits, waits to hit,
Despair is while festooned in the space,
Deadly askance dainty can as will drape,
Clever brass put on a brave chubby face,
A juicy sweet fruit is always a grape.
And when floating rubble as a bubble,
As the snake is with carnivorous hood,
Aspirant work a day school is a stubble,
The thin tartar race was with hackles stood,
Before laugh your lips can lively smack,
Put to death you can but and finely hack.

214
Yacht

Yacht is not at all a shaky phantom,
One more truth, one Achilles heel stimulate,
Auspicious vivacity was quantam,
Like a nip in the bud to mulate,
As emulsion that drums as to dwindle,
If you try the chance is only a stance,
And let us earn not to highly swindle,
When puckering as angry instance,
Negative approach is very awkward,
Gentle genialty stands for exhibition,
Sacking the good news remains as backward,
While the dotage is for some prohibition,
Neither purity nor paucity stern,
Everything ends in a green and fresh fern.

215
Headache

Headache can denote a noted sad nip,
Rather an aperture in a nasty tip,
Now my food is just a meagre tea sip,
May be that you are a party chief whip,
Some noble love encourages lipping,
Aloof radicalism amiss is rim,
Like a have or stag spotted high skipping,
Tall talk nonsense stringent alike keen swim,
Moreover syphoned or on time phoned,
For a cock tamed the name is a hackle,
Though fermented spirit spilt milk is toned,
New sample the hull you cannot well tackle,
Spilling and filling can cause negation,
Yet it is better than relegation.

216
Edict

No more despicable are the old hags,
Over the crags on and on run the stags,
Man can run three legged race in cold rags,
Like a beetle not to cringe or cleave the bags.
We are of course, caprice selfish capture,
As my is rather simply free hold,
Though in the bad blood it is in rapture,
High drama naize or burlesque and bold,
God fathers and demigods or scribes prescribe,
For they fail to malign and describe,
On a plaque the edict can inscribe,
Novelty that can no longer proscribe,
Indians are not philistine flear flimsy,
Artistry is in the flood not clumsy.

217
Catastrophe

Master creates now a happy new crisis,
Like Basil underwood under basil,
It is perhaps cremative basis,
Something great as rich as an old fossil.
Forensic medicines excel the mint,
For we may not fast in the latest lent,
And a formula is not perhaps a tent,
Cherubs have no proud bad presumption,
John the Baptist can save us all and fly,
So topsy-turvy crooked description,
Bold but guilty, however, churning and shy,
Sterile or virile our fate serves a gait,
And further more at times it is a trait.

218
Calumniation

In many cases satire is an attire,
Though a quarter well furnished,
And calumniation can also retire,
Yet is not splendid and burnished,
To prove or reprove (the) enunciation,
If feverish you maximise the tax,
Lampoons cannot lead to den for fax,
No picture is for release on lense,
On healthy grounds we cannot seduce,
Like philosophical dicta may cease,
Any image the cutlery can reduce,
Some apothecary shall feat announce,
As sergrant can reply or renounce.

219
Witches

Turf or surf can buffer the depression,
A Pandora's box opens for dejection,
Can also lead to utter repression,
Caste-worn turpitude treats on rejection.
Like a mismatch deluding redirection,
Unlike deep mine to palliate smoky ban,
Madness succumbs to feigned deduction,
A reptile is horrendous someone's fan,
As though a zero hero is a man,
Lashing and brittle although with less span,
Repulsive compulsion and little as tan,
Some alligators and the buck-rams ran,
In a land of dogs and clever bitches,
There is also a band of nice witches.

220
Transmutation

Nasty but angry flaccid and flabby,
Simple and master gloomy and bloaming,
May be that quilt is worn and not shabby,
Divisive clammy lamps are but looming,
Like longevity sphere is a sharp spear,
Leceration to cut and thrust or tear,
Though placid yet we are not barley clear,
Indian minds saddled in anguished fear.
Choosy, lazy, fazed changed with waste sheer,
Our tracks need not be glorious hanky-panky,
If so shaken gangsterism is mere,
Young girls fondly like young teachers cranky,
Seamly melange that suits the fine shanks,
Conciliating tantrums are now wide tanks.

221

Lynx

Acrimonious denoument wipes the brow,
The bad blood of sundry dreams can seeds sow,
Cat like cat-fish cannot just jig or crow,
Like the thundering thunderbolts are now,
Rendering meandering glow hampers,
Jogging and bogging that overpowers the prow,
Catching up with the match that tampers,
Friends do wonders I wonder, I fairly tracus,
Sunny funny atmosphere you can hanker,
And a monstrous double speak is a speak,
Dog days in summer we need a tanker,
Cover or discover you might feel angry check,
I know man is a two legged, of course, lynx,
And endearment stands as a strange sphinx.

222
Health

Undiscovered incongruous apt death,
Unlike a tall-grown thick oat or bad beach,
Some winter may not pour in living breath,
That can breach a noble Indian safe leech,
Rains came with altogether rhetoric and speech,
And not an ordinary man can teach,
A mad cap has no map nor selfless beach,
And also the emotions can highly screech,
Dirty body rings sings and then flinging,
Heroic hooliganism of a clown,
Subdued as debut a choice alone clings,
A froward fellow ilk can finely frown,
In India volteface is not a big stealth,
For we all live for a good cheerful health.

223
Chance

Full time job for a part time love is grace,
Sculpture on an edict we can trace,
Almost even scuff of a scudding brace,
Like the dimpled agony charming face,
A macerated ever green chubbing mace,
Flimsy brocade is a shining lace.
Soft is the hardship if in crafty space,
At long last like wise vampire can chase,
Hemp is unkempt too big a facial chance,
No freezing no tubid clear windy ramp,
Indian culture relevant Godly trance,
A scamp is a noted marvellous vamp,
It I comprehend as well apprehend,
As you can't do so you reprehend.

224
Revenge

A pot boiler hippopotamus can sink,
Ostensible young mind hardly to wink,
Vipers are critical showy to link,
A vibrating sound cards abundantly clink,
The ostentations gaga is reputed,
Pleonasm though a miasma segregated,
Rouge or siege is synergy deputed,
Like you and me wanna segregated,
Placid, lucid and taciturn but frank,
Sagacity, new velocity grand,
Thirsty agony and glory of a crank,
No indignant Godhead is a new brand,
Modern and active jig or peg madly speak,
An old revenge quakes treaks and mouse squeaks.

225
Double Speak

Double speak of groove marks the forceful task,
Woman cannot be honest so to host,
Husky as warmth in the sun we bark,
Like often the blockade rocks the rich toast,
Inasmuch as in astute and simple,
Night mavish many nightqueens are frigid,
The face is damaged by the pimple,
Fruits are mellow but not that rigid,
Ample tragic mindful of the fitment,
Free from the garbage is habitation,
Meticulous and warning of hutment,
Is the risk of changing capitation,
Any brittle temperature is fragile,
Though languishing as safe and agile.

226
Newness

Newness is in my hungry living palm,
Purport is though a silent stormy balm,
The pulpit spasmodic is hungry calm,
Like lonely kine stubbing as in the farm,
Around a heifer flies if angry swarm,
Starch as stock naked aloft rendition,
Obscurity forbears recondite harm,
Bankers also hanker the condition,
Encouraging desirous square squeezing,
Duplication of peeling the sweet charm,
Stay or stray on for funny freezing,
A tram and a ram cannot some way arm,
Impute to refute the way of tanning,
Sinners are prone to untimely scanning.

227
Porridge

In any soil a snake can truly coil,
It is our fate perhaps you and I toil,
Wonderful cleopatra alone can foil,
Though the blood within is to pry and boil,
As if pristine Indian culture were sweet,
Even the beasts can produce warmth and heat,
Succinet avowal may trample with feet,
And we know a horseman can as well beat,
After minced the sheep one for fine meat,
Something like prorridge is for no pouring,
Like a scowl for bowl if we cannot treat,
When sapine we are for a sound snoring,
A persona can shape all others fear,
A healthy hearing aid can help us hear.

228
Onyx

Onyx for Venus,
And emerald for Mahavir,
Thirthankaras know the fact,
Like know how for the secrecy,
Of life, strife and fife,
As in a profitable trade,
Jejune candelabrum,
Settler the complex matter.

Salvation as *Kaivalya*,
Like a dyer does that,
A magical mystery drooping,
Cooping up, onto intake,
Konpara is for stage show,
And that grief is yet brief,
Long love worn striptease,
Some cabaret eloquent,
No shipyard is for docking.

229
Tangible

A tangible Goddess, recalcitrant,
Magnifies the world,
Like a grail legend,
Fragment adulteration,
Reconnoiters the condour,
A tangent lug touching,
As in a touch and go,
Miracles one safe.

Conjoins and enjoins,
The trouble shooter shorn,
Like a sibling undertrial,
Conscription humanised,
Honeymoons before wedding,
Bedding, shedding tears,
Hersy New Jersy,
Some mackintosh,
And that is life infact!

230
Polytheism

Like an omniscient Goddess,
Venus is everywhere,
Nowhere, somewhere,
A potent well-wisher,
Be Konpara or Khajuraho,
Though emanciated lugebrious,
No dismal tide can shake,
She is a star indefinite.

Thawing and pawning,
Ludicrous to believe,
Like an environment favours,
One God, two Gods, Many Gods,
And a Third Front hails,
Failes, sails, trails holy,
Subdued, imbused, confused,
Venus is eternal,
A grail legend.

231
Fitment

Fatehpur Sikri,
With fitments and hutments,
Like all around weaning,
A webbed paw jibes,
And a claw too astir,
Veracious truthful deeds,
As "verdurous gloom",
Rather sunny settlements.

Figment as fitment,
We live for others mercuric,
Man protests woman,
Woman protects man,
Like anchoring truthful,
No tricksters, no turncoats,
When they float and waft,
India is great,
"Mera Bharat Mahan".

232
Greenery

Greenery, tannery,
With no appellation,
No jurisdiction,
Lo! no enjoyment in cuckoos song,
Like the song bird dreadful,
Owls are better than wnews,
Ravenous vultures veracious,
Read no books, exchange looks.

Like no chanotherapy,
Or even sight seeing,
Sing a little pleasant songs,
And at least cawing to zoo,
A melody turns to be malady,
Man's gestulations worsen,
Better than feminine gestures,
A shrew or muff does so,
Greenery is awry.

233
Sequestered Love

Sequestered love is simple,
A dimple in the cheek,
Like a cheeky glory freak,
Meek is the story,
For an elaborate recollection,
Sandwitched in a cream,
No chicanery or so,
Uneven seduction cuts off.

"Dutta, dayadhvam, damayata",
Gory visage sent, down we went,
"Marie hold on tight",
If we donned it is good,
No bra, no draw, no drought,
Love in an open rain,
Summer is over, springing,
Swing or sing or bring love,
"All are gone old familiar faces".

234
Themis

Themis is there,
For Tithone's bead ready,
Like the beadles for a prayer,
Justica and Jupiter,
Annotate Zeus,
For quoted quotables,
Thetis or priam,
Apollo as God of Wisdom.

Atmospheric pressure,
Fission for cushion,
Like confused fusion,
Quarrelsome nature is,
Powerful prowess,
And Godly fights,
Or the menace of cockroaches,
Though a dance favours them,
Whirlwind is the galaday.

235
No Matter

If man cowers no meaning,
Or a woman cowls no matter,
Like subdued serenity in fact,
Words can "embalm and treasure up",
Then up! up! my friends,
The winter is very near,
Aaran's rod can't fear,
Ablujas sing aloud.

As unknown figure-head,
Mewling and 'pucking' in nurses arms,
Like the armistice composed,
Peace of utrecht classical,
Standards can buy and sell,
On roughing up ruffians shine,
Glitter and twitter,
May be a smattering,
No matter of funeral orations.

236
Quilt

Belt is felt as a quilt,
With no guilt, a strong paw,
And a cat's paw,
Like a felt cap anew,
A feeling on fathers day,
A probable catechism,
Cataclysm or symbolism,
A literary jargon high.

Catchy words impressive,
Like secret phalli cult,
Render or meander strange,
Whimsical preamble encore,
Cataracts as cascade,
Lead to discourse perforce,
A bridal sings for praise,
Absurd or meaningful,
Also but dissolution.

237
Lashing

Lashing, barking and crashing,
Are common in fife,
Like a wife that can do,
Fire flies and gun battles,
Can make India great,
Now it is the other way out,
Squatting, fasting to chastise,
Echo in the type or hype.

Cleverness is all,
Since the monsoon fails or falls,
Like a classical rain batters,
Of Puranas or God sent ire,
We are in the cistern or pattern,
We are silent to speak out,
A proud bride is chaste,
Though in haste she can sulk,
The ilk is better half.

Short Poems

238

May God save us all,
Medicos and medicines,
Perhaps will help us.

239

India is a great gem,
For her vastness genial,
Also bread and butter.

240

Seduce and produce,
Mothers and brides know it well,
And all that we trow.

241

Water flows or glows,
It is but maritime range,
We all know it well.

242

Foreshadows pulpit,
Rex, Bentex or syntex sells,
History they make.

243

Nature subsides spell,
It is subsidiary lull,
A local poncho.

244

Seer the stamina,
And you will wonder aimful,
No one is shameful.

245

Over production,
Is also good soft spoken,
If not rotten eggs.

246

I hate Osmania,
But I love Kakatiya,
Both are nice two fold.

247

Padding and adding,
Poetry is at door step,
Sometimes good or bad.

248

Cowships are nice yet,
After all flowers they are,
Benign, delicate.

249

Frustrated you are!
Frustration will end your life,
Stagecraft and statecraft.

250

Snatey, sneakish folk,
Hornbill cannot kill us so,
It flummoxes leads.

251

Harry Potter is,
Among the foxes, vixen,
Not a wanderer.

252

Of sticks and broomsticks,
Indian culture sustains now,
Bugging and mugging.

253

Sometimes unusual words,
Look askance or askens,
or for sashaying.

254

You are a gung-ho,
For your matters hold gunge on,
Hold in or holdout.

255

To tilt the guilty,
Ilk is a silk for milk bulk,
The significance.

256

There is a problem,
And also its solution,
Since India is great.

257

For a hug or lug,
Confusion or infusion,
We can write and writhe.

258

Lovers meet for love,
They meet and mate for their fate,
Or for an offspring.

259

Each periphery,
I remember if it were,
And hostile fellows.

260

Blank forgetfulness,
Orphanage is a better den,
Uncompromising.

261

Persecution still,
History is a mystery,
So prosecution.

262

I live fine India,
Mavericks are also good,
God will forgive me.

263

Because they are good,
Indians do not denigrate,
They are full of beans.

264

No vehemence yet,
For a characterless group,
may be a charade.

265

Old man and the Sea,
Some Courage for me remains,
Let us help others.

266

Tenets like linnets,
swerve and fly for heaven,
For camouflage.

267

No honest man lives,
Survives or sustains as beings,
And India is great.

268

One echoes the other,
And individuation grows,
Personality cult.

269

Who will bell the cat?
I believe every fellow,
A perfect gentleman.

270

You can't change the world,
I think I can do a little,
You are a braggart.

271

Divert or invert,
You can desist a large thing,
Larger in the scope.

272

The world is wanton,
And fractured publicity,
Our Gods and legends!

273

Only God is great,
Indian are free from deceit,
So nobody is great.

274

Sleep well or leap well,
God is always great for us,
No depredations!

275

Upper class Gods sulk,
No sloth but appeasement,
Propiate Gods.

276

Acclimatize,
New acclimatization,
Viewpoints vary.

277

Meaningful song dot,
Indian morals are superb,
For they love each other.

278

Stamps and ramps protrude,
Above human animals,
A land of morale!

279

Aceteus is author,
As an originator old,
Combines old and new.

280

No vibes, only jibes,
Like an orientation comes,
So we live by chance.

281

Defiant of nature,
Like an equity share,
I am always safe.

282

Despair to repair,
Human seasons or reasons,
Repair to despair.

283

A hen and a cock,
Sleep or weep together well,
They need a fine niche.

284

Fireflies or butterflies,
And the centaur hotels new,
Can never make glue.

285

Heaven born rampant,
Primordial or dead arrows,
Every caste is great.

286

Malange or melce,
Both are mellifluous gifts,
Though melancholic.

287

At times we are good,
Grab the opportunity,
Man close to man.

288

No qualms for us now,
Pleasure seeking animals,
Palliate the goodness.

289

Perspicacity,
Industrial mechanism,
Puddle is much low.

290

Diluted dimness,
Salutation needs revolt,
Extravaganza.

291

Mind set up permits,
Through thick and thin a trio in,
And skin is a proof.

292

Net work or pet work,
It is a social tragedy,
Prow and vow and crow.

293

Within or without,
Alacrity is stable,
It is tour-de-force.

294

Indians as beggars,
Not all the same but a few,
Angels and devils.

295

Body language speaks,
Slaves fight for their master,
Freakish crooks and brooks.

296

Public are ruffians,
They like only cajoling,
Perhaps volition.

297

Seminacks and cracks!
Everyone is not rogue,
Stupid is trot.

298

Struggle or giggle,
You are yourself not rotten,
Ramage is the same.

299

Stout may also spout,
It is self-aggrandisement,
Or Herald Tribune.

300

I write for myself,
Or even for you at times,
Indian trade cycles.

301

Everyday has rain,
As something goes asunder,
Altwart in the sky.

302

No scurrilities,
Scurrying or worrying,
I don't know much.

303

Little presentiment,
Anything is for hire and fire,
Nothing is askew.

304

I am a druggist,
You are for apt eucharist,
Sole solemnity.

305

Border Mizoram,
Stands as a face of India,
Or even buckram.

306

Tetchy folk I know,
Some last vilification,
Everyone is grim.

307

Indians make money,
For themselves or for none,
Only to castigate.

308

Hallucination is God,
Ratiocination is God,
Everything is God,
Nothing is God,
As something is God.

309

Like munificent eminence,
The reticence grows,
As an embodiment,
Of the fire works ebullient,
Can grace the disgrace.

310

Man is an animal,
Animal is man,
Snowman, stoneman, concman,
Like chicanery upheld,
An embryonic wealth.

311

People are cunning,
But they are winning,
And running for death,
Like the dying moths,
It is moth hour now.

312

Rules change to help the fools,
And the mules or the palfreys,
Like the gulging whelps,
Or a metrical romance,
For even a symbiosis.

313

We mull null and void,
Something willy nilly,
Like nagging braggarts,
Or gulls as wagtails,
That is enough.

314

For self-abnegation,
A dog in the manger,
Like a phantam that growls,
Tolls or rallies apart,
Mulls and lulls.

315

Penetrating venerable,
Sound and fury,
Like the mildew overpowering,
Crosses the stilts,
In depth psychology.

316

Woman was man's chattel,
But now she is a partner,
Like the enslaved freedom,
As in qualified monism,
That extols nature and stature.

317

Not to adjudicate the justice,
For Supreme Judge is God,
And we live for mundane things,
Like the persistent gravity,
Simplicity is the present thief.

318

As a part of the history,
We forget the mystery,
Like a jumbo jet,
The oblivion occupies,
That is the human brain.

319

From will to will-power,
Like will-o-the-wisp,
Man is overbunded in life,
Perhaps only to decay in fray,
But is is almost a paragon.

320

Indian minds are fair,
Like window panes and blinds,
For they forget sins fast,
And look forward ahead,
For no new crimes and plans.

321

Bragging and dragging,
Man is a careerist alone,
Like a perseverant simplicity,
Man is God and God is man,
There can be no touch-and-go.

322

Breakfast or speak fast,
Death comes to us at last,
Like chagrined migraine,
Mountains cannot meander,
Only the rivers do a little.

323

God is everywhere,
God is nowhere,
God is somewhere,
Centre of the universe,
Reverse or even adverse.

324

From deluge to tillage askew,
The mushroom growth of poetry,
Like the every day fight,
On the certain death,
To bite the dust.

325

Biting cold and winter blues,
Blow, blow then winter winds,
Some speech is read,
To break the ice,
Or to face it.

326

Formally we cut no ice,
Cherished or perished,
Like sneaking pecking,
Climax is the source,
Await the tombstone.

327

First comes love,
Then comes lad the next,
Follows the doll or creched,
Like the pegasm of the sky,
Or the Arabian Night Stories.

328

Shadowy thoughts,
As about chamera,
Moods and deeds implore,
Like stucco construction,
We build castles in the air.

329

Live and let live,
Even in tsunami land,
Rains and floods aplamb,
Like acute shortage,
We blow hot and cold.

330

Spill the beans,
(Reveal the secret),
Like a choking voice,
Or Cleopatra's nose (needle?),
None will bell the cat.

331

Prurient and pristine sex,
May be a psychiatric cult,
Nature plays mischief,
Even for a trousseau,
Like law and order judgement.

332

There is government,
There is people's government,
There is also leader's government,
Of kitchen cabinet,
And also kitchen queens.

333

Indian minds,
Refined and confined,
Like volatile stimuli,
Look for the pinpricks,
Paeans and godmen.

334

Ramping with shampoo,
As a childish behaviour,
Like a good reticence,
And marketing is costly,
Systems play with us.

335

Wife is a chief whip,
With mandatory order,
Like howling foxy winds,
Dogged to death,
Fall on no deaf ears.

336

Life is a large cruise,
No ramp but a little huff,
Like a big ample bruise,
It's a glorious stuff.

337

Astitute are solid things,
Like destitute smears,
The harbinger that brings,
For us stored are tears.

338

As sallow or fallow,
Satire is the far best,
Like the water shallow,
Behest is the zest.

339

Women can also fight,
Like the byte for site,
It they are very bright,
Grooming croning then might.

340

Like throttled wattle,
Is chugging or bugging,
Rattle of a battle,
Some lugger is lugging.

341

Purloined are the loins,
Besmeared with the part,
Like aesthetics and coins,
No doubt forever they last.

342

Window blinds, Indian minds,
Corn out of fine tillage,
As concotion that binds,
Animonious pillage.

343

Gentle waft of the wind,
Full circle of the spring,
Like the elite and rind,
We bring only to cling.

344

Indian standards lo!
They are just great, nonsense,
Like spoken English no?
And credentials are there.

345

Newsmongers, warmongers,
Carte blanche create,
Claptrap or some lap-tap,
Dead-end like a hearse,
Sanity smears the truth.

346

Human minds are not migs,
We are all but single,
Like the barrels and kegs,
The puppy styles mingle.